Turner

W. Cosmo Monkhouse

Alpha Editions

This edition published in 2024

ISBN : 9789362516473

Design and Setting By
Alpha Editions
www.alphaedis.com
Email - info@alphaedis.com

As per information held with us this book is in Public Domain.
This book is a reproduction of an important historical work. Alpha Editions uses the best technology to reproduce historical work in the same manner it was first published to preserve its original nature. Any marks or number seen are left intentionally to preserve its true form.

Contents

PREFACE. ....- 1 -
CHAPTER I. INTRODUCTORY. ....- 3 -
CHAPTER II. EARLY DAYS. 1775 TO 1789. ....- 6 -
CHAPTER III. YOUTH. 1789 to 1796. ....- 15 -
CHAPTER IV. YORKSHIRE AND THE YOUNG
ACADEMICIAN. 1797 TO 1807..- 26 -
CHAPTER V. THE LIBER STUDIORUM—HIS POETRY AND
DRAGONS. ....- 36 -
CHAPTER VI. HARLEY STREET, DEVONSHIRE,
HAMMERSMITH, AND TWICKENHAM. 1800 TO 1820. .- 48 -
CHAPTER VII. ITALY AND FRANCE. 1820 TO 1840. ......- 59 -
CHAPTER VIII. LIGHT AND DARKNESS.
1840 TO 1851. ....- 78 -
FOOTNOTES: ....- 92 -

PREFACE.

THE late Mr. Thornbury lost such an opportunity of writing a worthy biography of Turner as will never occur again. How he dealt with the valuable materials which he collected is well known to all who have had to test the accuracy of his statements; and unfortunately many of the channels from which he derived information have since been closed by death. Mr. Ruskin, who might have helped so much, has contributed little to the life of the artist but some brilliant passages of pathetic rhetoric. Overgrown by his luxuriant eloquence, and buried beneath the *débris* of Thornbury, the ruins of Turner's Life lay hidden till last year.

Mr. Hamerton's "Life of Turner" has done much to remove a very serious blot from English literature. Very careful, but very frank, it presents a clear and consistent view of the great painter and his art, and is, moreover, penetrated with that intellectual insight and refined thought which illuminate all its author's work.

He has, however, left much to be done, and this book will, I hope, help a little in clearing away long-standing errors, and reducing the known facts about Turner to something like order. To these facts I have been able to add a few hitherto unpublished; and it is a pleasant duty to return my thanks to the many kind friends and strangers for the pains which they have taken to supply me with information. To Mr. F. E. Trimmer, of Heston, the son of Turner's old friend and executor; to Mr. John L. Roget; to Mr. Mayall, and to Mr. J. Beavington Atkinson, my thanks are especially due.

In so small a book upon so large a subject, I have often had much difficulty in deciding what to select and what to reject, and have always preferred those events and stories which seem to me to throw most light upon Turner's character. On purely technical matters I have touched only when I thought it absolutely necessary. This part of the subject has been already so well and fully treated by Mr. Ruskin in numerous works, too well known to need mention; by Mr. Hamerton in his "Life of Turner," and "Etching and Etchers;" by Messrs. Redgrave in their "Century of English Painters," and by Mr. S. Redgrave in his introduction to the collection of water-colours at South Kensington, that I need only refer to these works such few among my readers as are not already acquainted with them. I would also refer them for similar reasons to Mr. Rawlinson's recent work on the "Liber Studiorum."

I should have liked to add to this volume accurate lists of Turner's works and the engravings from them, with information of their possessors, and the extraordinary fluctuation in the prices which they have realized, but this would have entailed great labour and have swelled unduly the bulk of this volume, which is already greater than that of its fellows. Fortunately this information is likely to be soon supplied by Mr. Algernon Graves, whose accurate catalogue of Landseer's works is sufficient guarantee of the manner in which he will perform this more difficult task.

The edition of Thornbury's "Life of Turner" referred to throughout these pages, is that of 1877.

W. COSMO MONKHOUSE.

CHAPTER I.

INTRODUCTORY.

THE task of writing a satisfactory life of Turner is one of more than usual difficulty. He hid himself, partly intentionally, partly because he could not express himself except by means of his brush. His secretiveness was so consistent, and commenced so early, that it seems to have been an instinct, or what used to be called by that name. Akin to the most divinely gifted poets by his supreme pictorial imagination, he also seems on the other side to have been related to beings whose reasoning faculty is less than human. When we look at such pictures as *Crossing the Brook*, *The Fighting Téméraire*, and *Ulysses and Polyphemus*, we feel that we are in the presence of a mind as sensitive as Keats's, as tender as Goldsmith's, and as penetrative as Shelley's; when we read of the dirty discomfort of his home and of the difficulty with which his patrons, and even his relations, obtained access to his presence—how even his most intimate friends were not admitted to his confidence—we can only think of a hedgehog, whose offensive powers being limited, is warned by nature to live in a hole and roll itself up into a ball of spikes at the approach of strangers.

We are used to having our idols broken; but we still fashion them with a persistency which seems to argue it a necessity of our nature, that we should think of the life and character of gifted men as being the outward and visible sign of the inward and spiritual grace we perceive in their works. It is this habit which makes any attempt to write a life of Turner pre-eminently unsatisfactory, for his refined sense of the most ethereal of natural phenomena is not relieved by any refinement in his manners, his supreme feeling for the splendour of the sun is unmatched by any light or brilliance in his social life; his extreme sensibility, a sensibility not only artistic but human, to all the emotional influences of nature, stands for ever as a contrast to his self-absorbed, suspicious individuality. There is of course no reason why a landscape painter should be refined in manner or choice in his habits. There is no necessary connection between the subjects of such an artist and himself, except his hand and eye. He lives a life of visions that may come and go without affecting his life or even his thought, as we generally use that word. The most tremendous phenomena of nature may be seen and studied, and reproduced with such power as to strike terror into those who see the picture, and yet leave the artist unaltered in demeanour and taste. Even those men of genius who, instead of employing their imagination upon nature's inanimate works, devote themselves to the study of man himself, socially and morally, do not by any means show that relation between themselves and their finest work that we appear naturally to expect.

But all this, though it may explain much, still leaves unsatisfactory the task of writing the life of a man of whom such passages as the following could be sincerely written:—

"Glorious in conception—unfathomable in knowledge—solitary in power—with the elements waiting upon his will, and the night and morning obedient to his call, sent as a prophet of God to reveal to men the mysteries of the universe, standing, like the great angel of the Apocalypse, clothed with a cloud, and with a rainbow upon his head, and with the sun and stars given into his hand."—*Modern Painters* (1843), p. 92.

"Towards the end of his career he would often, I am assured on the best authority, paint hard all the week till Saturday night; and he would then put by his work, slip a five-pound note into his pocket, button it securely up there, and set off to some low sailor's house in Wapping or Rotherhithe, to wallow till Monday morning summoned him to mope through another week."—THORNBURY'S *Life of Turner* (1877), pp. 313, 314.

The contrast is too great to make the picture pleasant, the facts are too few to make it perfect; to make it one or the other, it would be necessary to do as Turner did, and rightly did, with his perfect drawings—suppress facts that jarred with his scheme of form and colour, and insert figures or mountains or clouds that were necessary to complete it; but a biography is nothing if not real—it belongs to the other side of art. The task would be rendered lighter, if not more agreeable, if we were frankly to accept the principle of a dual nature, and cutting up our subject into halves, treat Turner the artist and Turner the man as two separate beings; and there would, at first sight, seem to be no more convincing proof of this duality than is afforded by Turner. He had an exquisitely sensitive apprehension of all physical phenomena, and was able to hoard away his impressions by the thousand in that wonderful brain-store of his, until they were wanted for pictures. He stored them with his eye, he reproduced them with his hand and memory. These three were all of the finest, and seemed to act without that process which is necessary to most of us before we can make use of our impressions, viz., the translation of them into words. This process is as necessary for the nourishment of most minds as digestion for the nourishment of the body, but to him it appears to have been almost entirely denied. He had grasp enough of his impressions without it, to enable him to analyze them and compose them pictorially; but he could not give any account of them or of his method of composition, and they had no sensible effect on his conversation.

He thus lived in two worlds—one the pictorial sight-world, in which he was a profound scholar and a poet, the other the articulate, moral, social word-world in which he was a dunce and underbred. In the one he was great and happy, in the other he was small and miserable; for what philosophy he had was fatalist. The riddle of life was too hard for his uncultivated intellect and starved heart to contemplate with any hope; he was only at rest in his dreamland. When he came down into this world of ours from his own clouds, he brought some of his glory with him, but without any cheerful effect; for it came but as a foil to ruined castles, the vice of mortals and the decay of nations.

Yet, while at a first view this distinction between Turner as a man and Turner as an artist seems complete, further study shows that the man had a great and often a fatal influence on the artist, and that this was not without reaction both serious and deep, and so we find that his art and himself are no more to be divided in any human view of him than were his body and his soul when he was yet alive. For these reasons we shall keep as close together as possible the histories of his life and his art, a task always difficult and sometimes impossible on account of the scantiness of trustworthy data for the one and the almost infinite material for the other.

CHAPTER II.

EARLY DAYS.

1775 TO 1789.

THE appearance of Turner's genius in this world is not to be accounted for by any known facts. Given his father and his mother, his grandfather and grandmother, on the father's side, which is all we know of his ancestry, given the date of his birth, even though that was the 23rd April (St. George's day, as has been so childishly insisted on), 1775, there seems to be positively no reason why William Turner, barber, of 26, Maiden Lane, opposite the Cider Cellar, in the parish of St. Paul's, Covent Garden, and Mary Turner, *née* Marshall, his wife, should have produced an artist, still less, one of the greatest artists that the world has yet seen. There is only one fact, and that a very sad one, which might be held to have some connection with his genius. "Great wits are sure to madness near allied," sang Dryden,[1] and poor Mrs. Turner became insane "towards the end of her days." This, however, will in no way account for the special quality of Turner's genius. He arose like many other great men in those days to help in opening the eyes of England to the beauties of nature, one of the large and illustrious constellation of men of genius that lit the end of the last and the beginning of the present century, and with that truth we must be content.

The earliest fact that we have on record which had any influence on Turner is that his paternal grandfather and grandmother spent all their lives at South Molton in Devonshire. Although he is not known to have visited Devonshire till he was thirty-seven years of age;[2] he appears to have been proud of his connection with the county, and to have asserted that he was a Devonshire man. This is, as far as we know, the solitary effect of Turner's ancestry upon him. Of his father and mother the influence was necessarily great. From his father he undoubtedly obtained his extraordinary habits of economy, that spirit of a petty tradesman, which was one of his most unlovely characteristics, and, be it added, his honesty and industry also. Of his father we have several descriptions by persons who knew him; of his mother, one only, and that, unfortunately, not so authentic. We will give the lady the first place, and it must be remembered that this unfavourable picture is drawn by Mr. Thornbury from information derived from the Rev. Henry Syer Trimmer, the son of Turner's old friend and executor, the Rev. Henry Scott Trimmer, of Heston, who obtained it from Hannah Danby, Turner's housekeeper in Queen Anne Street, who got it from Turner's father.

"In an unfinished portrait of her by her son, which was one of his first attempts, my informant perceived no mark of promise; and he extended the same remark to Turner's first essays at landscape. The portrait was not wanting in force or decision of touch, but the drawing was defective. There was a strong likeness to Turner about the nose and eyes; her eyes being represented as blue, of a lighter hue than her son's; her nose aquiline, and the nether lip having a slight fall. Her hair was well frizzed—for which she might have been indebted to her husband's professional skill—and it was surmounted by a cap with large flappers. Her posture therein (*sic*) was erect, and her aspect masculine, not to say fierce; and this impression of her character was confirmed by report, which proclaimed her to have been a person of ungovernable temper, and to have led her husband a sad life. Like her son, her stature was below the average."

This as the result of a painted portrait by her son, and verbal description by her husband, is not too flattering, and it is all we know of the character and appearance of poor Mary Turner. Of her belongings we know still less. She is said to have been sister to Mr. Marshall, a butcher, of Brentford, and first cousin to the grandmother of Dr. Shaw, author of "Gallops in the Antipodes," and to have been related to the Marshalls, formerly of Shelford Manor House, near Nottingham.[3] We are able to add to this scanty information that she was the younger sister of Mrs. Harpur, the wife of the curate of Islington, who was grandfather of Mr. Henry Harpur, one of Turner's executors. He (the grandfather) fell in love with his future wife when at Oxford, and their marriage brought her sister to London. We are also informed that the hard-featured woman crooning over the smoke, in an early drawing by Turner in the National Gallery (*An Interior*, No. 15), is Turner's mother, and the kitchen in which she is sitting, the kitchen in Maiden Lane. We have also ascertained that one Mary Turner, from St. Paul's, Covent Garden, was admitted into Bethlehem Hospital on Dec. 27th, 1800, one of whose sponsors for removal was "Richard Twenlow, Peruke Maker." This unfortunate lady, whether Turner's mother or not, was discharged uncured in the following year. Altogether what we know about Turner's mother does not inspire curiosity, and we fear that she was never destined to figure in an edition of "The Mothers of Great Men." The "sad life" which she is said to have led her husband could scarcely have been sadder than her own.

Of his father we have fuller information.

"Mr. Trimmer's description of the painter's parent, the result of close knowledge of him, is that he was about the height of his son, spare and muscular, with a head below the average standards" (whatever that may mean) "small blue eyes, parrot nose, projecting chin, and a fresh complexion indicative of health, which he apparently enjoyed to the full. He was a chatty old fellow, and talked fast, and his words acquired a peculiar transatlantic twang from his nasal enunciation. His cheerfulness was greater than that of his son, and a smile was always on his countenance."

This description is of him when an old man, but he must have been not very different from this when about one year and eighteen months after his marriage, which took place on August 29th, 1773, the little William was born. He was not a man likely to alter much in habit or appearance. He was always stingy, if we may judge by the story of his following a customer down Maiden Lane to recover a halfpenny which he omitted to charge for soap, and from his son's statement that his "Dad" never praised him for anything but saving a halfpenny. As barbers are proverbially talkative, and as persons do not generally develop cheerfulness in later life, we may consider Mr. Trimmer's portrait of the old man to be essentially correct of him when young, especially as we find that Turner the younger was always "old looking," a peculiarity which is generally hereditary.

The house (now pulled down) in which Turner was born, and in which, for at least some time after, father, mother, and son resided together, is thus described by Mr. Ruskin: "Near the south-west corner of Covent Garden, a square brick pit or well is formed by a close-set block of houses, to the back windows of which it admits a few rays of light. Access to the bottom of it is obtained out of Maiden Lane, through a low archway and an iron gate; and if you stand long enough under the archway to accustom your eyes to the darkness, you may see, on the left hand, a narrow door, which formerly gave access to a respectable barber's shop, of which the front window, looking into Maiden Lane, is still extant." Maiden Lane is not a very brilliant thoroughfare, and was still narrower and darker at this time, but still this picture, though doubtless accurate, seems to make it still darker, and in the engraving of the house in Thornbury's life of Turner, even the front window that looked into Maiden Lane is rendered ominously black by the shadow of a watchman thrown up by his low-held lantern. To us it seems that there is plenty of dark in Turner's life without thus unduly heightening the gloom of his first dwelling-place. A barber cannot do his work without light, and we have no doubt that whatever sorrow fell upon Turner in his life was in no way deepened by his having to pass through a low archway and an iron gate in order to get to his father's shop.

HOUSE IN MAIDEN LANE IN WHICH TURNER WAS BORN.

The house in Maiden Lane would have been a cheerful enough and a wholesome enough nest for little William[4] if it had contained a happy family presided over by a sweetly smiling mother. This want is the real dark porch and iron gateway of his life, the want which could never be supplied. In that wonderful memory of his, so faithful, by all accounts, to all places where he had once been happy, there was no chamber stored with sweet pictures of the home of his youth; no exhaustless reservoir of tender, healthy sentiment, such as most of us have, however poor. Here is a note of pathos on which we might dwell long and strongly without fear of dispute or charge of false sentiment. Children, indeed, do not miss what they have not: present sorrows did not probably affect his appetite, future forebodings did not dim his hopes; but then, and for ever afterwards, he was terribly handicapped in the struggle for peace and happiness on earth, in his desire after right thinking and right doing, in his aims at self-development, in his chance of wholesome fellowship with his kind, in his capacity for understanding others and making himself understood, for all these things are more difficult of attainment to one who never has known by personal experience the charm of what we mean by "home."

This want in his life runs through his art, full as it is of feeling for his fellow-creatures, their daily labour, their merry-makings, their fateful lives and deaths; there is at least one note missing in his gamut of human circumstance—that of domesticity. He shows us men at work in the fields, on the seas, in the mines, in the battle, bargaining in the market, and carousing at the fair, but never at home. This is one of the principal reasons why his art has never been truly popular in home-loving domestic England.

It is not good for man, still less for a boy, to be alone, and we do not think we can be wrong in thinking that he was a solitary boy. How soon he became so we do not know. We may hope that in his earliest years at least he was tenderly cared for by his mother, and petted by his father. There is no reason why we may not draw a bright picture of his childhood, and fancy him walking on Sundays with his father and mother in the Mall of St. James's Park, wearing a short flat-crowned hat with a broad brim over his curly brown hair, with snowy ruffles round his neck and wrists, and a gay sash tied round his waist, concealing the junction between his jacket-waistcoat and his pantaloons; but this bright period cannot have lasted long. Soon he must have been driven upon himself for his amusement, and fortunate it was for him that nature provided him with one wholesome and endless.

It is known that one artist, Stothard, was a customer of his father, and it is probable that as there was an academy in St. Martin's Lane, and the Society of Artists at the Lyceum, and many artists resided about Covent Garden, the little boy's emulation may have been excited by hearing of them, and perhaps chatting with them and seeing their sketches.

He certainly began very early. We are told that he first showed his talent by drawing with his finger in milk spilt on the teatray, and the story of his sketching a coat-of-arms from a set of castors at Mr. Tomkison's the jeweller, and father of the celebrated pianoforte maker, must belong to a very early age.[5] The earliest known drawing by him of a building is one of Margate Church, when he was nine years old, shortly before he went to his uncle's at New Brentford for change of air. There he went to his first school and drew cocks and hens on the walls, and birds, flowers, and trees from the school-room windows, and it is added that "his schoolfellows, sympathizing with his taste, often did his sums for him, while he pursued the bent of his compelling genius." Very soon after this, if not before, he began to make drawings, some of these copies of engravings coloured, which were exhibited in his father's shop window at the price of a few shillings, and he drew portraits of his father and mother, and of himself at an early age. It is said that his father intended him to be a barber at first,[6] but struck with his talent for drawing soon determined that he should follow his bent and be a painter. He is said to have delighted in going into the fields and down the river to sketch, but all the very early drawings we have seen, including those purchased at his father's shop, are drawings of buildings, mostly in London. Of these there is one of the interior of *Westminster Abbey*, in Mr. Crowle's edition of "Pennant's London," now in the print room of the British Museum. There is nothing to distinguish these from the work of any clever boy, but this drawing and one in the National Gallery, of a scene near Oxford, both probably copied from prints, show a sense not only of light but colour. We have also seen a copy of Boswell's "Antiquities of England and Wales," with about seventy of the plates very cleverly coloured by him when a boy at Brentford.

Whatever defects Turner, the barber, may have had as a father, neglect of his son's talents was not one of them, and, though very careful for the pence, he showed that he could make a pecuniary sacrifice when he had a chance of furthering his son's prospects, for he refused to allow him to become the apprentice of one architect who offered to take him for nothing, and paid the whole of a legacy he had been left to place him with another, and we may presume a better one.

The information given by Mr. Thornbury about his early training, scholastic and professional, is very meagre, inconsecutive, and puzzling. According to him it was in 1785 that Turner, having been previously taught reading, but not writing, by his father, went to his first school, which was kept by Mr. John White, at New Brentford; in 1786 or 1787, by which time at least his destination for an artist's career appears to have been settled, he was sent to "Mr. Palice, a floral drawing-master," at an Academy in Soho, and in 1788, to a school kept by a Mr. Coleman at Margate; at some time before 1789, to Mr. Thomas Malton, a perspective draughtsman, who kept a school in Long Acre, and in this year to Mr. Hardwick, the architect, and to the school of the Royal Academy. He also went to Paul Sandby's drawing school in St. Martin's Lane. During all, or nearly all this time, he was, according to Mr. Thornbury, employed: 1. In making drawings at home to sell. 2. In colouring prints for John Raphael Smith, the engraver, printseller, and miniature painter. 3. Out sketching with Girtin. 4. Making drawings of an evening at Dr. Monro's[7] in the Adelphi. 5. Washing in backgrounds for Mr. Porden. If he was really employed in this way from 1785 to 1789, and could only read and not write when he began this extraordinary course of training, it is no wonder that he remained illiterate all his life, or that his mind was utterly incapacitated for taking in and assimilating knowledge in the usual way. Spending a few months at a day school, and a few more at a "floral drawing master," then a few more at school at Margate, making drawings for sale, colouring prints, fruitlessly studying perspective, bandied about from school master to drawing master, and from drawing master to architect—such a life for a young mind from ten to fourteen years of age is enough to spoil the finest intellectual digestion.

One fact, however, comes clear out of all this confusion, that of regular and ordinary schooling he had little or none, and there is no reason to suppose that it was because of the peculiar quality of his mind that he always spoke and wrote like a dunce. He never had a fair chance of acquiring in his youth more than a traveller's knowledge of his own language, and so his mind had a very small outlet through the ordinary channels of speech. On the other hand, faculties of drawing and composition were trained to the utmost, and this compensated him in a measure. His mind had only one entrance, his eye, and only one exit, his hand; but they were both exceptional, and cultivated exceptionally.

CHATEAU D'AMBOISE.
From "Rivers of France."

There was, however, much of pleasure in this life for a boy like Turner, for though he evidently worked hard, he liked work and the work he had to do was especially congenial to him. He met friends and encouragers on all sides; from his father to his school-fellows. However much reason he may have had for disappointment in later years, there was none in his early life. He was "found out" in his childhood. Encouraged by his father, with his drawings finding a ready sale to such men as Mr. Henderson, Mr. Crowle, and Mr. Tomkison, with plenty of employment in no slavish mean work for such a youngster, such as colouring prints and putting in backgrounds to drawings, with Mr. Porden generously offering to take him as an apprentice for nothing, with a kind friend like Dr. Monro always willing to give him a supper and half-a-crown for sketches of the country near his residence at Bushey, or the result of an evening's copying of the then best attainable water colours; his life was far more agreeable, far more tended to make him think well of the world and of the people in it than has been usually represented, and probably as good as he could have had for attaining early proficiency in his art. London at that time was not a bad place for a landscape artist. It was neither so clouded nor so sooty as it is now; there were healthier trees in it, and more of them, a more picturesque and a purer river, and within less than half an hour's walk from Maiden Lane there were green fields, for north of the British Museum the country was still open.

But he was not entirely dependent upon his art and his employers for enjoyment, or for forming his opinion of the human race. There were houses at which he visited and where he was received warmly. When at school at Margate he got an "introduction to the pleasant family of a favourite schoolfellow;" at Bristol there was Mr. Narraway,[8] a fellmonger in Broadmead, and an old friend of his father, at whose house he drew two of the children and his own portrait; and at the house of Mr. William Frederick Wells, the artist, he was evidently one of the family, as is proved by the charmingly tender reminiscences of Mrs. Wheeler.

"In early life my father's house was his second home, a haven of rest from many domestic trials too sacred to touch upon. Turner loved my father with a son's affection; and to me he was as an elder brother. Many are the times I have gone out sketching with him. I remember his scrambling up a tree to obtain a better view, and then he made a coloured sketch, I handing up his colours as he wanted them. Of course, at that time, I was quite a young girl. He was a firm affectionate friend to the end of his life; his feelings were seldom seen on the surface, but they were deep and enduring. No one would have imagined, under that rather rough and cold exterior, how very strong were the affections which lay hidden beneath. I have more than once seen him weep bitterly, particularly at the death of my own dear father,[9] which took him by surprise, for he was blind to the coming event, which he dreaded. He came immediately to my house in an agony of tears. Sobbing like a child, he said, 'Oh, Clara, Clara! these are iron tears. I have lost the best friend I ever had in my life.' Oh! what a different man would Turner have been if all the good and kindly feelings of his great mind had been called into action; but they lay dormant, and were known to so very few. He was by nature suspicious, and no tender hand had wiped away early prejudices, the inevitable consequence of a defective education. Of all the light-hearted merry creatures I ever knew, Turner was the most so; and the laughter and fun that abounded when he was an inmate of our cottage was inconceivable, particularly with the juvenile members of the family."—THORNBURY'S *Life of Turner* (1877), pp. 235, 236.

A man who knew this lady for sixty years, and about whom so kind a heart could have thus written, could not have been driven to a life of morbid seclusion because the world had treated him so badly in his youth. His home may have been, and probably was a cheerless one, and we may well pity him on that account. The rest of our pity we had better reserve for his want of education, and the secretive, suspicious disposition which nature gave him, and which he allowed to master his more genial propensities.

CHAPTER III.

YOUTH.

1789 to 1796.

THE only rebuff with which the young artist appears to have met was from Tom Malton, the perspective draughtsman, who sent him back to his father as a boy to whom it was impossible to teach geometrical perspective. As Mr. Hamerton observes, "There is nothing in this which need surprise us in the least. Scientific perspective is a pursuit which may amuse or occupy a mathematician, but the stronger the artistic faculty in a painter the less he is likely to take to it, for it exercises other faculties than his. Besides this, he feels instinctively that he can do very well without it." No doubt he did feel this, and the feeling very much lessened the disappointment at being "sent back," and he did very well without it, so well that he was appointed Professor of Perspective to the Royal Academy without it, and not unfrequently exhibited pictures on its walls, which showed how very much "without it" he was.

Otherwise he met with no rebuffs in his art. We have seen that he got plenty of employment, and have expressed an opinion that that employment—colouring engravings, and putting in backgrounds and foregrounds and skies for architectural drawings—was no mean employment for a youngster. He himself, when pitied in later years for this supposed degradation and slavery, replied, "Well, and what could be better practice!" and it was this and more. It not only taught him to work neatly, to lay flat washes smoothly and accurately, but it taught him to exercise his ingenuity and artistic taste. He probably succeeded so well, because it gave him an opportunity of displaying his artistic faculty. Every sketch that he had thus to beautify presented an artistic problem, how best to light and decorate and make a picture of the bare bones of an architectural design. It gave him a sense of power and importance thus to be the converter of topography into art; it taught him the value of light and shade, and the decorative capacities of trees and sky. His success gave him self-reliance. It also, and this was perhaps a more doubtful advantage, taught him to consider drawing as a skill in beautifying. He got the habit of treating buildings as objects less valuable as objects of art in themselves, than for the breaking of sunbeams, and as straight lines to contrast with the endless curves of nature; and also the habit of using trees as he wanted them, of bending their boughs and moulding their contours in harmony with the poem-picture of his imagination. To this early treatment of architectural drawings may be traced his great power of composition, and also much of his mannerism.

That he soon knew his power, and had his secrets of manipulation, may be one reason for his early secretiveness about his art; for though there is little in these early works of his to prefigure his coming greatness, he, when a youth, attained a proficiency equal to that of the best water-colour artists of his day, and, with his friend Girtin, soon surpassed all except Cozens; and he could not have done this without a sense of superiority and many private experiments; or, on the other hand, he may, like many men, have required complete solitude to work at all, though this was not the case in later life, as he often painted almost the whole of his pictures on the Academy walls. At all events, the degree of his secretiveness is extraordinary. "I knew him," says an old architect, "when a boy, and have often paid him a guinea for putting backgrounds to my architectural drawings, calling upon him for this purpose at his father's shop in Maiden Lane, Covent Garden. He never would suffer me to see him draw, but concealed, as I understood, all that he did in his bedroom." When in this bedroom one morning, the door suddenly opened, and Mr. Britton entered.[10] In an instant Turner covered up his drawings and ran to bar the crafty intruder's progress. "I've come to see the drawings for the Earl."[11] "You shan't see 'em," was the reply. "Is that the answer I am to take back to his lordship?" "Yes; and mind that next time you come through the shop, and not up the back way." When Mr. Newby Lowson accompanied him on a tour on the continent he "did not show his companion a single sketch." Similar stories could be added to show how this habit continued through his life.

The dates of these two early stories are not given by Mr. Thornbury, nor the name of the "old architect," but they show that he was early employed by a nobleman, and that he got a guinea a piece for his backgrounds, not only "good practice," but good pay for a youth; he was, in fact, better employed and better paid than any young artist whose history we can remember. Nor does it seem to have been the fault of Providence if he did not enjoy the crowning happiness of life, a friend of suitable tastes, for Girtin was sent to him, a youth of his own age endowed with similar gifts, and of a most sociable disposition; nor did he want a capable mentor, for he had Dr. Monro, "his true master," as Mr. Ruskin calls him.

It was at Raphael Smith's that he formed an intimacy with Girtin, says Mr. Alaric Watts.[12] "His son, Mr. Calvert Girtin, described his father and young Turner as associated in a friendly rivalry, under the hospitable roof and superintendence of that lover of art, Dr. Monro (then residing in the Adelphi). Nor was Turner forgetful of the Doctor's kindness, for on referring to that period of his career, in a conversation with Mr. David Roberts, he said, 'There,' pointing to Harrow, 'Girtin and I have often walked to Bushey and back, to make drawings for good Dr. Monro, at half-a-crown apiece and a supper."'

If a saying quoted by T. Miller in his "Memoirs of Turner and Girtin" may be trusted,[13] Turner may have met Gainsborough and other eminent painters of the day at Dr. Monro's. Speaking of Dr. Monro's conversaziones, "Old Pine, of 'Wine and Walnuts' celebrity, used to say, 'What a glorious coterie there was, when Wilson, Marlow, Gainsborough, Paul, and Tom Sandby, Rooker, Hearne, and Cozins (*sic*) used to meet, and you, old Jack,' turning to Varley, 'were a boy in a pinafore, with Turner, Girtin, and Edridge as bigwigs, on whom you used to look as something beyond the usual amount of clay.'" As Gainsborough died in 1788, when Turner was thirteen years old, and Turner was only two years the senior of John Varley, this shows how early he began to have a reputation.

The acquaintance between Turner and Girtin is one of the most interesting facts in Turner's Life. Being more than two years Turner's senior (Girtin was born on February 18th, 1773) and having at least equal talent as a boy, it is probable that he was "ahead" of Turner at first, and that Turner learnt much from him. We may therefore accept as true his reputed sayings, "Had Tom Girtin lived, I should have starved;"[14] and (of one of Girtin's "yellow" drawings), "I never in my whole life could make a drawing like that, I would at any time have given one of my little fingers to have made such a one."[14] With regard to their mutual studies and their respective talents we have information in the studies and drawings themselves, but with regard to their human relationship we have very little. Turner always spoke of him as "Poor Tom," and proposed to, and possibly did, put up a tablet to his memory; but there are no letters or anecdotes to show that what we all mean by "friendship" ever existed between them.

We are equally ignorant as to the amount of intimacy between him and Dr. Monro, for though the latter did not die till 1833, there is nothing to show that they ever met after Turner's student days were over.

It may, however, be fairly assumed that we should have known more about his intimacy with his Achates and his Mæcenas if it had been great and continuous. The absence of documents or rumours on the subject are all in favour of his having kept himself to himself, of his absorption in his art from an early date, neglecting the social advantages that were open to him, neglecting intellectual intercourse with his artistic peers, neglecting everything except the pursuit of his art, and the road to wealth and fame. This self-absorption, this concentration of all his time and power to this one but triple object, the trinity of his desire, may have arisen from a natural cause, the strength of impelling genius over which he had no control; it may have arisen from secretiveness, suspicion, selfishness, and ambition, which he could have controlled but would not; but whatever its cause, there is no doubt that it existed, and that with every external facility for becoming a social and cultivated being, he took the solitary path which led him to greatness (not perhaps greater than he might have otherwise attained), but a greatness accompanied with mental isolation and ignorance of all but what he could gather from unaided observation, and an uncultivated intellect.

The education of Turner may be summed up as follows: he learnt reading from his father, writing and probably little else at his schools at Brentford and Margate, perspective (imperfectly) from T. Malton, architecture (imperfectly and classical only) from Mr. Hardwick, water-colour drawing from Dr. Monro, and perhaps some hints as to painting in oils from Sir Joshua Reynolds, in whose house he studied for a while. The rest of his power he cultivated himself, being much helped by the early companionship of Girtin. Nearly all, if not all, this education except that mentioned in the last paragraph was over in 1789, when Sir Joshua laid down his brush, conscious of failing sight, and young Turner became a student of the Royal Academy.

NANTES.
From "Rivers of France."

These were his principal living instructors, but he learnt more from the dead—from Claude and Vandevelde, from Titian and Canaletto, from Cuyp and Wilson. He learnt most of all from nature, but in the beginning of his career his studies from art are more apparent in his works. There is scarcely one of his predecessors or contemporaries of any character in water-colour painting that he did not copy, whose style and method he did not study, and in part adopt. We have within the last few years only been able to study at ease the works of the early water-colour painters of England, and the result of the interesting collections now at South Kensington and the British Museum, bequests of Mr. and Mrs. Ellison, Mr. Towshend, Mr. William Smith, and Mr. Henderson, has been on the one hand to increase our opinion of their merit, and on the other to show how far Turner outstripped them. We can now see how true and delicate were the lightly-washed monochrome water scenes of Hearne; how robust the studies of Sandby; that Daniell and Dayes could not only draw architecture well, but could warm their buildings with sun, and surround them with space and air; that Cozens could conceive a landscape-poem, and execute it in delicate harmonies of green and silver; that Girtin could invest the simplest study with the feeling of the pathos of ruin and solemnity of evening; the first of water-colour painters to feel and paint the soft penetrative influence of sunlight, subduing all things with its golden charm. In looking at one of his drawings now at South Kensington, a *View of the Wharfe*, and comparing it with the works around, one cannot help being struck with this difference, that it is complete as far as it goes, the realization of one thought, the perfect rendering of an impression, harmonious to a touch. Broad and almost rough as it is, it is yet finished in the true sense as no English work of the kind ever was before. There are more elaborate drawings around, plenty of struggle after effects of brighter colour, much cleverness, much skill, but nowhere a picture so completely at peace with itself. In looking at it we can realize what Turner meant when he said that he could never make drawings like Girtin. Equal harmony of tone, far greater and more splendid harmonies of colour, miracles of delicate drawing, triumphs over the most difficult effects, dreams of ineffable loveliness, very many things unattempted by Girtin he could achieve, but never this simple sweet gravity, never this perfection of spiritual peace.

But in spite of this, the great fact in comparing Turner with the other water-colour painters of his own time—and we are speaking now of his early works—is this, that whereas each of the best of the others is remarkable for one or two special beauties of style or effect, he is remarkable for all. He could reach near, if not quite, to the golden simplicity of Girtin, to the silver sweetness of Cozens; he could draw trees with the delicate dexterity of Edridge, and equal the beautiful distances of Glover; he could use the poor body-colours of the day, or the simple wash of sepia, with equal cleverness. He was not only technically the equal, if not master of them all, but he comprehended them, almost without exception.

Such mastery was not attained without extraordinary diligence in the study of pictures. At Dr. Monro's he could study all the best modern men, including Gainsborough, Morland, Wilson, and De Loutherbourg, and he could also study Salvator Rosa, Rembrandt, Claude, and Vandevelde. One day looking over some prints with Mr. Trimmer,[15] he took up a Vandevelde and said, "That made me a painter." And Dayes (Girtin's master) wrote in 1804:—"The way he acquired his professional powers was by borrowing where he could a drawing or a picture to copy from, or *by making a sketch of any one in the Exhibition[16] early in the morning, and finishing it at home.*" The character of his early works is sufficient of itself to prove the extent of his study of pictures, and we are inclined to think that most of his early practice was from works of art, and not from nature. The spirit of rivalry commenced in him very early; it was the only test of his powers, and he seems to have pitted himself in the beginning of his career against all his contemporaries, from Mr. Henderson to Girtin, and many of the old masters, and never to have entirely relinquished the habit. When we think of the number of years he spent in doing little but topographical drawings, a castle here, a town there, an abbey there, with appropriate figures in the foreground, using only sober browns and blues for colours, his progress seems to have been very slow; but when we see most of the artists of his time doing exactly the same, and that the old landscape painters whom he principally studied were almost as limited in the colours they employed, especially in their drawings, we do not see how he could well have progressed more quickly; and when we further consider the enormous distance which he travelled—from the very bottom to the very height of his art—that he should have accomplished it all in one short life appears miraculous. The milestones of his journey are not shown plainly in his early work, that is all.

That there was much conscious restraint on his part in the use of colours, that he of wise purpose devoted himself to perfection of his technical power before he endeavoured to show his strength to the world, we see no reason to believe. He could not well have done otherwise, and for such an original mind one marvels to observe how throughout his career he was led in the chains of circumstance. The poet-painter, the dumb-poet, as he has well been called, shows little eccentricity of genius in his youth. There was the strong inclination to draw, but no strong inclination to draw anything in particular, or anything very beautiful. On the contrary, he drew the most uninteresting and prosaic of things, copied bad topographical prints and ugly buildings. When it was proposed to make him an architect he did not rebel; when it was afterwards proposed to make him a portrait-painter he did not murmur. It was Mr. Hardwick, not himself, that insisted on his going to the Royal Academy. His first essay in oils was due to another's instigation. Whatever work came to him, he did; that which he could do best, that which he had special genius for, the painting of pure landscape, he scarcely attempted at all for years. Almost every artist of that day went about England drawing abbeys, seats, and castles for topographical works. What others did, he did. What others did not do, he did not do. No doubt it was the only profitable employment he could get, and he very properly took it, and worked hard at it; he was borne along the stream of circumstance as everybody else is, but he, unlike most men of strong genius, seems never to have attempted to stem its tide, or get out of its way. His genius was a growth to which every event and accident of his life added its contribution of nourishment. Though stirred with unusual power, he was probably almost as unconscious as to what it tended as a seed in the ground; he had a dim perception of a light towards which he was growing; he was conscious that he put forth leaves, and that he should some day flower, but when, and with what special bloom he was destined to surprise the world, we doubt if he had any prophetic glimpse. His development was extraordinary, and could only have been produced by special careful training, but this training was mainly due to circumstances over which he had no control. Nature came to his assistance in a thousand different ways, and in nothing more than giving him a quiet temperament, like that of Coleridge's child, "that always finds, and never seeks." He was not fastidious, except with regard to his own work, and about that, more as to the arrangement and finish of it than the subject. He had an excellent constitution, early inured to rough it, and his comforts were very simple and easily obtained. He was not particular, even about his materials and tools; any scrap of paper would do for a sketch on an emergency. He was always able to work, and to work swiftly and well. No fidgeting about for hours and days because he was not in the mood; no sacrifice of sketch after sketch because they did not please him; none of that nervous restlessness which so often attends imaginative workers; and his work was imaginative from the first—if not in conception, in execution. Solitude seems to have been the only necessary condition for the free exercise of his powers, which were as happily employed in "making a picture" of one thing as of another, and when he wanted something to put in it to get it "right," he never had much trouble in finding it. He said, "If when out sketching you felt a loss, you have only to turn round, or walk a few paces further, and you had what you wanted before you." His physical powers were also great, and his mind was active in receiving impressions. Mr. Lovell Reeve, as quoted by Mr. Alaric Watts, says:—"His religious study of nature was such that he would walk through portions of England, twenty to twenty-five miles a day, with his little modicum of baggage at the end of a stick, sketching rapidly on his way all striking pieces of composition, and marking effects with a power that daguerreotyped them in his mind. There were few moving phenomena in clouds and shadows that he did not fix indelibly in his memory, though he might not call them into requisition for years afterwards." He was not tied to any particular method, or bound to any particular habit; when he found that his way of sketching was too minute and slow to enable him to make his drawings pay their expenses, he changed his style to a broader, swifter one. So, without going quite to the length of Mr. Hamerton, who appears to think that everything in Turner's youth (including ugliness and bandy legs) happened for the best in the best of possible worlds, we may safely affirm that he could scarcely have been gifted with a temperament better suited for steady progress, or one which was more calculated to make him happy, for it enabled him to exercise his body and mind at the same time, to earn his living and to lay up stores of pictorial beauty in his memory, to do whatever task was set him, and yet get artistic pleasure out of even the most commonplace study by embellishing it with his imagination.

In 1789 he became a student of the Royal Academy, and in the year after he exhibited a *View of the Archbishop's Palace at Lambeth*. In 1791, 2, and 3 he exhibited several topographical drawings, but down to this time he seems to have made no sketching tours of any length. He drew in the neighbourhood of London, and his journeys to stay with friends at Margate and Bristol will account for his drawings of Malmesbury, Canterbury, and Bristol. But about 1792 he received a commission from Mr. J. Walker, the engraver (who also afterwards employed Girtin), to make drawings for his "Copper-plate Magazine." This was the beginning of the long series of engravings from his works, and it may have been one of the reasons which decided him to set up a studio for himself, which he did in Hand Court, Maiden Lane, close to his father, where he remained till he was elected an Associate of the Royal Academy in 1800, when he removed to 64, Harley Street. A year or so after his employment by Walker he got similar commissions from Mr. Harrison for his "Pocket Magazine." These commissions sent him on his travels over England referred to by Mr. Lovell Reeve. The copper-plates of the sketches for Walker, including some after Girtin, were found about sixty years afterwards by Mr. T. Miller, who republished them in 1854, in a volume called "Turner and Girtin's Picturesque Views, sixty years since." These drawings mark his first tour to Wales, on which he set forth on a pony lent by Mr. Narraway. The first public results of this tour were the drawing of *Chepstow* in "Walker's Magazine" for November, 1794, and three drawings in the Royal Academy for that year. By the next year's engravings and pictures we trace him to "Nottingham," "Bridgnorth," "Matlock," "Birmingham," "Cambridge," "Lincoln," "Wrexham," "Peterborough," and "Shrewsbury," and by those of 1796 and 1797 to "Chester," "Neath," "Tunbridge," "Bath," "Staines," "Wallingford," "Windsor," "Ely," "Flint," "Hampton Court, Herefordshire," "Salisbury," "Wolverhampton," "Llandilo," "The Isle of Wight," "Llandaff," "Waltham," and "Ewenny (Glamorgan)," not including drawings of places he had been to before.

His furthest point north was Lincoln, his farthest west (in England) Bristol. The only parts in which he reached the coast were in Wales and the Isle of Wight. Lancashire and the Lakes, Yorkshire and its waterfalls, were yet to come, and nearly all coast scenery, except that of Kent.

The drawings for the Magazines were not remarkable for any poetry or originality of treatment perceptible in the engravings, the cathedrals being generally taken from an unpicturesque point of view, more with the object of showing their length and size than their beauty, to which he appears to have been somewhat insensible always; they show a great love of bridges and anglers—there is scarcely one without a bridge, and some have two; a desire to tell as much about the place as possible by the introduction of figures; they show his habit of taking his scenes from a distance, generally from very high ground, and his delight in putting as much in a small space as possible, and his power of drawing masses of houses, as in the *Birmingham* and the *Chester*.

The result of these tours may be said to have been the perfection of his technical skill, the partial displacement of traditional notions of composition, and the storing of his memory with infinite effects of nature. It was as good and thorough discipline in the study of nature, as his former life had been in the study of art, and though his visit to Yorkshire in the next year (1797) seemed necessary to bring thoroughly to the surface all the knowledge and power he had acquired, it was not without present fruit. Rather of necessity than choice, we may observe, he confined his powers mainly to the drawing of views of places supposed to be of interest to the subscribers of the Magazines, but his individual inclinations in the choice of subject, and his tendency to purer landscape and sea-view, showed themselves now and then. First in his drawing of *The Pantheon, the Morning after the Fire*, exhibited in 1792; next in 1793, in his *View on the River Avon, near St. Vincent's Rocks, Bristol*, and the *Rising Squall, Hot Wells*,[17] from the same place; then in 1794, *Second Fall of the River Monach, Devil's Bridge*; in 1795, *View near the Devil's Bridge, Cardiganshire, with the River Ryddol*; in 1796, *Fishermen at Sea*; and in 1797, *Fishermen coming Ashore at Sunset, previous to a Gale*, and *Moonlight: a study in Milbank*,[18] now in the National Gallery.

That his genius was perceptible even in these early days is evident from the notice taken in a contemporary review of his drawings in 1794, when he was nineteen.

"388. *Christchurch Gate, Canterbury*. W. Turner. This deserving picture, with Nos. 333 and 336, are amongst the best in the present exhibition. They are the productions of a very young artist, and give strong indications of first-rate ability; the character of Gothic architecture is most happily preserved, and its profusion of minute parts massed with judgment and tinctured with truth and fidelity. This young artist should beware of contemporary imitations. His present effort evinces an eye for nature, which should scorn to look to any other source."

Again in 1796, the "Companion to the Exhibition," with regard to his first sea-piece contains this paradoxical sentence, attempting to express his peculiar power of giving a distinct impression of ill-defined objects, which was apparently evident even in this early work.

"Colouring natural, figures masterly, not too distinct—obscure perception of the objects distinctly seen—through the obscurity of the night—partially illumined."

Again in 1797, we have this testimony as to the extraordinary (for that time) character of his work, from an entry in the diary of Thomas Greene, of Ipswich, about the *Fishermen* of 1797.

"June 2, 1797. Visited the Royal Academy Exhibition. Particularly struck with a sea-view by Turner; fishing vessels coming in, with a heavy swell, in apprehension of tempest gathering in the distance, and casting, as it advances, a night of shade, while a parting glow is spread with fine effect upon the shore. The whole composition bold in design and masterly in execution. I am entirely unacquainted with the artist; but if he proceeds as he has begun, he cannot fail to become the first in his department."

Here, then, before Turner's visit to Yorkshire, we have evidence that not only was the superiority of his work apparent, but that one or two of the special qualities which were to mark it in the future were already perceived, and publicly praised.

After looking carefully at all the ascertainable facts of Turner's youth, we can only come to the conclusion that it was not the fault of nature or mankind that he grew into a solitary and disappointed man.

Secretiveness on his own part and want of trust in his fellow-creatures seem to have been bred in him, and to have resisted all the many proofs which the friends of his youth, and we may say of his life, afforded, that there were kind and unselfish persons in the world whom he could trust, and who would trust him. There is no proof that he ever had confidential relations with any human being, not even Girtin. That he should have willingly cut himself adrift from human fellowship we are loath to believe, in spite of the many facts which seem to support it. It seems more natural, and on the whole (sad as even this is) more pleasant, to believe that he met with a severe blow to his confidence; that, though naturally suspicious, the many kindnesses he received were not without a gracious effect, but that his budding trust was killed by a sudden unexpected frost. For these reasons we are inclined to believe in the story of his early love; although it, as told by Mr. Thornbury, is not without inconsistencies.

Turner is said to have plighted vows with the sister of his school friend at Margate; he left on a tour, giving her his portrait, the letters between them were intercepted, and after waiting two years she accepted another. When he reappeared she was on the eve of her marriage, and thinking her honour involved, refused to return to her old love.

Such in short is the story which we wish to believe, and as it came to Mr. Thornbury from one who heard it from relatives of the lady, to whom she told it, there is probably some truth in it. It is, however, almost impossible to believe that Turner, whose tours never extended to two years, and whose power of locomotion was extraordinary, should allow that time to elapse without going to see one whom he really loved. If he did not get any letters he would have been desperate; if he did get letters they would have shown him that she had not received his, which would have made him, if possible, more desperate still. As the name of the lady is not given, it is next to impossible to find out the truth. Our faith, however, as a balance of probability, still remains that Turner was jilted, and that the effect of it was to confirm for ever his want of confidence in his fellow-creatures.

CHAPTER IV.

YORKSHIRE AND THE YOUNG ACADEMICIAN.

1797 TO 1807.

FHE the facts of the foregoing chapter it may be fairly presumed that although Turner's election as Associate in 1799 followed quickly after his fine display of pictures from the northern counties in 1798, he was before this a marked man, whose superiority over all then living landscape painters was visible to critics and lovers of art, and could not have been disguised from the eyes of the artists of the Royal Academy. It did not require a genius like that of Turner to distance competitors on the Academy walls in those days. England was almost at its lowest point both in literature and art. The great men of the earlier part of the eighteenth century, Pope, Thomson, Gray, Collins, Swift, Fielding, Sterne and Richardson, had long been dead, and of the later brilliant, but small circle of artists and men of letters of which Dr. Johnson was the centre (Goldsmith and Burke, Garrick and Reynolds, Hume and Gibbon), Reynolds only was left, and he was moribund. Of other artists with any title to fame there was none left but De Loutherbourg and Morland; Hogarth had died in 1764, Wilson in 1782, Gainsborough in 1788. The new generation of men of genius were born; some were growing up, some in their cradles. A few had already shown signs. Wordsworth and Coleridge had just put forth their "Lyrical Ballads" at Bristol, Burns was famous in Scotland, Charles Lamb had written "Rosamund Gray," but Scott the "Great Unknown," was as yet "unknown" only, though five years older than Turner; Byron had not gone to Harrow, and the united ages of Keats and Shelley did not amount to ten years; the only living poets of deserved repute were Cowper and Crabbe. Della Crusca in poetry, and West in art, were the bright particular stars of this gloomy period. The landscape painters who were Academicians were such men as Sir William Beechey, Sir Francis Bourgeois, Garvey, Farington, and Paul Sandby, and among the Associates, Turner had no more important rival than Philip Reinagle. Girtin and De Loutherbourg alone of all the then exhibitors were anything like a match for him, and Girtin spoilt (till 1801) any chance he might otherwise have had of Academic honours by not exhibiting pictures in oil; he died in 1802, leaving Turner undisputed master of the field. It is not greatly therefore to be wondered at that Turner was elected Associate in 1799, and a full Academician in 1802. It was, however, much to the credit of the Academy that they recognized his talent so soon and welcomed him as an honour to their body, instead of keeping him out from jealous motives. Turner never forgot what he owed to the Academy, and whether it taught him nothing, as Mr. Ruskin says, or a great deal, as Mr. Hamerton thinks, does not much matter—it taught him all it knew, and gave him ungrudgingly every honour in its gift. But its claims on his gratitude did not stop here, for it was his school in more than one branch of learning; from its catalogues he derived the subjects of most of his pictures, they directed him to the poems which set flame to his imagination, and helped (unfortunately), with their queer spelling and grammar and truncated quotations, to form what literary style he had; but the greatest boon which the Academy afforded was the opportunity of fame, a field for that ambition which was one of the ruling powers of his nature.

But his tour in the North in 1797 was before his days of Academic rivalries and glories. He was only two-and-twenty, and seems to have been actuated by no motive but to paint as well and truly as he could the beautiful scenery through which he passed. The effect upon him of the fells and vales of Yorkshire and Cumberland seems to have been much the same as that of Scotland upon Landseer; it braced all his powers, developed manhood of art, turned him from a toilsome student into a triumphant master. Mr. Ruskin writes more eloquently than truly about this first visit. "For the first time the silence of nature around him, her freedom sealed to him, her glory opened to him. Peace at last, and freedom at last, and loveliness at last; it is here then, among the deserted vales—not among men; those pale, poverty-struck, or cruel faces—that multitudinous marred humanity—are not the only things which God has made." These are fine words, but what a picture, if true! Can this young man who has travelled through all these many counties in England and Wales, which we have already enumerated, never have known the "silence of nature," or "freedom," or "peace," or "loveliness?" Can his experience of mankind, of Dr. Monro, of Girtin, of Mr. Hardwick, of Sir Joshua Reynolds, of Mr. Henderson, have left upon him such an impression of the failure of God's handiwork in making men, that a mountain seems to him in comparison as a revelation of unexpected success? If Turner had been cooped in a garret of the foulest alley in London since his birth, and had only escaped now and then from the hardest drudgery to read the works of Mr. Carlyle, this picture might be near the truth, but we doubt even then if it could escape the charge of being over-coloured.

Whether Turner had any special object in this journey to the North in 1797 is not clear, but it is at least probable that Girtin's success at the Exhibition of this year with his drawings from Yorkshire and Scotland may have influenced him, and that he may have already received a commission from Dr. Whitaker to make drawings for the "Parish of Whalley," published three years afterwards. He must at all events have had much leisure from other employment in order to produce the important pictures in oil and water-colour which he exhibited the next year. Of these we only know *Morning on the Coniston Fells* and *Buttermere Lake*, now in the National Gallery. Another, whether water or oils we do not know, was *Norham Castle on the Tweed—Summer's Morn*, the first of several pictures of the same subject, which was a favourite of his for a good reason. Many years after (probably about 1824 or 1825), when making sketches for "Provincial Antiquities and Picturesque Scenery of Scotland, with descriptive illustrations by Sir Walter Scott, 1826," he took off his hat to Norham Castle, and Cadell the publisher, who was with him, expressed surprise. "Oh," was the reply, "I made a drawing or painting of Norham several years since. It took; and from that day to this I have had as much to do as my hands could execute." If the Castle was treated in the same way in this first as in the subsequent pictures of Norham, with the hill and ruin in the middle distance set against a brightly illumined sky, the effect was sufficiently new and striking to make the reputation of any painter in those days. It was an effect which as far as we know had never been attempted before, this casting of the whole shadow of hill and castle straight at the spectator, so that, in spite of the bright reflections in the watery foreground, he seems to be within it, and to see through the soft shadowy air, the solemn bulk of mound and ruin, with their outlines blurred with light, grand and indistinct against the burning sky.

NORHAM CASTLE, ON THE TWEED.

The pictures of 1797-99 confirmed beyond any doubt that a great artist had arisen, who was not only a painter but a poet—a poet, not so much of the pathos of ruin, though so many of his pictures had ruins in them, nor of the chequered fate of mankind, though there is something of the "Fallacies of Hope" indicated in the quotations to his pictures—as of the mystery and beauty of light, of the power of nature, her inexhaustible variety and energy, her infinite complexity and fulness. No one can look upon his splendid drawing of *Warkworth Castle*, exhibited in 1799, and now at South Kensington, with its rich glow of sunset and transparent shadow, and its wonderful masses of clouds, without feeling that such work as this was a revelation in those days. Sparing and not very pleasant in colour, it is yet in this respect a great advance upon the former work of others and of his own; such colour as there is penetrates the shade and is complete in harmony and tone, while the sky has no blank space and is part of the picture, the vivifying uniting power of the composition, with more interest and feeling in one roll of its truly-studied masses of cloud-form than could be found in the whole of any sky of his contemporaries.

Altogether it is difficult to over-estimate the influence of this first journey to the North upon Turner's mind and art, although he had almost perfected his skill and shown unmistakable signs of genius before. But these tours had other gifts not less important, though in a different way, for his introductions to Dr. Whitaker, the local historian, to Mr. Basire, the engraver, to Mr. Fawkes of Farnley, to Lord Harewood, and to Sir John Leicester (afterwards (1826) Lord de Tabley), through Mr. Lister-Parker of Browsholme Hall, his guardian, may all be said to have resulted from this tour.

Dr. Whitaker was the vicar of the parish of Whalley, and was writing a book upon it in the manner of those days, giving descriptions of the local antiquities, the churches, the ruins, the crosses, and an account of the county families, with their pedigrees and engravings of their ancestral seats. Not only each county, but almost every parish had such a historian in those days, and although the spirit of these works is archaeological rather than artistic, engaged with genealogy rather than history, and with pride of family and county rather than of the people and nation, they did a great deal of valuable work. Dr. Whitaker's work is no exception to this rule, and he was in many ways a typical writer of the kind, for he himself, though he "chose" the Church as his profession, was a man of property and county importance. Valuable as artists were in those days to the writers of these works, they were yet considered of very secondary rank. They were indeed not called "artists" but "draftsmen," and notwithstanding that Dr. Whitaker recognized Turner's genius, he did not think it necessary in this "Parish of Whalley" to mention in the preface the existence of such a person, although the names of all the gentlemen of the county who had furnished him with drawings or information are carefully acknowledged therein; but nothing will show better the relations between the two men than an extract from a letter from the reverend bookmaker to one of his county friends, Mr. Wilson, of Clitheroe, dated Feb. 8th, 1800.

"I have just had a ludicrous dispute to settle between Mr. Townley" (Charles Townley, Esq. of Townley), "myself and Turner, the draftsman. Mr. Townley it seems has found out an old and very bad painting of Gawthorpe at Mr.

Shuttleworth's house in London, as it stood in the last century, with all its contemporary accompaniments of clipped yews, parterres, &c.: this he insisted would be more characteristic than Turner's own sketch, which he desired him to lay aside, and copy the other. Turner, abhorring the landscape and contemning the execution of it, refused to comply, and wrote to me very tragically on the subject. Next arrived a letter from Mr. Townley, recommending it to me to allow Turner to take his own way, but while he wrote, his mind (which is not unfrequent) veered about, and he concluded with desiring me to urge Turner to the performance of his requisition, as from myself. I have, however, attempted something of a compromise, which I fear will not succeed, as Turner has all the irritability of youthful genius."[19]

The "compromise" was handing over the task of drawing from the objectionable picture to Mr. J. Basire the engraver.

We should like to see Turner's "tragical" letter, and also his rejected drawing; we should also like to have seen Dr. Whitaker's face if he had been told that not many years after a book would have been published of drawings by Turner, the draftsman, with "descriptions by the Rev. Dr. Whitaker."

Of Mr. Fawkes, of whose hall at Farnley Turner made a drawing for the "Parish of Whalley," but with whom he is said by Thornbury to have become acquainted about 1802, it may be said that he was one of Turner's longest and staunchest friends. The number of drawings (still at Farnley) which he made when visiting Mr. Fawkes between 1803 and 1820 (including as they do studies of birds shot while he was there, of the outhouses, porches, and gateways on the property, of the old places in the vicinity, and of the rooms in Farnley Hall) attest the frequency of his visits and his affection for the place and its occupants, while the splendid series of drawings in England, Switzerland, Italy, and on the Rhine, and the few precious oil pictures purchased by Mr. Fawkes, show him to have been not only a true friend, but a warm and sympathizing admirer of his genius. He indeed was a friend such as few are permitted to know—one of a goodly number who in Turner's youth and manhood should have made the world to him specially pleasant and sociable, frank and healthy. If he could not or would not have it so, it was not from insensibility, for his feeling was deep and his heart was sound. "He could not make up his mind to visit Farnley after his old friend's death," and he could not speak of the shore of the Wharfe (on which Farnley Hall looks down) "but his voice faltered." Dayes wrote of him in 1804, "This man must be loved for his works, for his person is not striking, nor his conversation brilliant." At Farnley, as at Mr. Wells' cottage, Turner was made at home, but that he did not escape good-humoured ridicule even at Farnley is plain from a caricature by Mr. Fawkes, "which is thought by old friends to be very like. It shows us a little Jewish-nosed man in an ill-cut brown tail coat, striped waistcoat, and enormous frilled shirt, with feet and hands notably small, sketching on a small piece of paper, held down almost level with his waist."[20] It is evident that at this time, in spite of his clear little blue eyes, and his small hands and feet, his appearance was not one likely to prepossess women, or to inspire consideration among men, and that one of the ills from which his painting room afforded a refuge may have often been a wounded vanity. There can be nothing more constantly galling to a sensitive man of genius than to feel that his appearance does not inspire the respect he feels due to him. If he has eloquence sufficient to command attention, this will not matter so much; but if he has not even that (and Turner had not), his natural refuge is solitude, his one absorbing occupation is his art, his only worldly ambition is to show what is in him, and to compel respect to his genius through his works.

From the time that Turner became an Associate his struggles, if he can ever be said to have had any, were over, and many changes took place in his life and art. He ceased almost entirely from making topographical drawings for the engravers, limiting his efforts to a heading to the "Oxford Almanack," and a few drawings for "Britannia Depicta," "Mawman's Tour," and some other books, until the commencement of the "Southern Coast" in 1814. He had in effect emancipated himself from "hackwork," and could turn his attention to more congenial and ambitious labour. The "draftsman" had become the artist, and he showed the improvement in his position by moving from Hand Court, Maiden Lane, to 64, Harley Street.

In future his exhibited pictures show very few "castles" or "abbeys," unless they are the seats of his distinguished patrons, Mr. Beckford of Fonthill (for whom in 1799 he painted several views of that ill-fated tower, which might have formed a subject for a canto of Turner's "Fallacies of Hope"), Sir J. L. Leicester, and others. His other castles, Carnarvon, 1800, Pembroke, 1801 and 1806, St. Donat's, 1801, and Kilchurn, 1802, were all probably compositions in which local fidelity was cared for little in comparison with effects of light and pictorial beauty. How completely he disregarded local fact in the case of Kilchurn has been very completely shown by Mr. Hamerton, and Mr. Ruskin says, "Observe generally, Turner never, after this time, 1800, drew from nature without *composing*. His lightest pencil sketch was the plan of a picture, his completest study on the spot a part of one."

Of this period, 1800-1810, Mr. Ruskin says, "His manner is stern, reserved, quiet, grave in colour, forceful in hand. His mind tranquil; fixed in physical study, on mountain subject; in moral study, on the Mythology of Homer, and the Law of the Old Testament." We wish he had given his reasons for this last astonishing statement. For those who only know the working of Turner's mind through his pictures, it is bewildering in the extreme, for in these there is no trace that he ever at any time studied the Law of the Old Testament, and the only classical pictures of this period, including the plates in the

"Liber," were *Jason* and *Narcissus and Echo*. If we include the pictures of 1811, we get one Homeric subject, *Chryses*, but that has nothing to do with mythology.

The evidence of Turner's pictures shows little tranquillity of mind during this period, but, on the contrary, all the restlessness of unsatisfied ambition. As he had already pitted himself against, and beaten all the water-colourists, he now commenced a course of rivalry against all the oil painters past and present, who came anywhere within the reach of his art, which he endeavoured to extend far beyond landscape limits.

His first tilt was probably against De Loutherbourg in 1799 with his *Battle of the Nile, at ten o'clock, when the l'Orient blew up, from the station of the gunboats between the battery and Castle of Aboukir*, and his *Fifth Plague of Egypt* (1800), his *Army of the Medes destroyed in the Desert by a Whirlwind*, and *The Tenth plague of Ægypt* (1802), probably owed more to De Loutherbourg's grand but theatrical pictures and *Eidophusicon*, than to any meditation on the "Law of the Old Testament."[21] Of Wilson, though dead, and neglected even when alive, he continued in active rivalry as late as 1822, when he proposed to Mr. J. Robinson, of the firm of Hurst and Robinson, to have four of his pictures (three of which were to be painted expressly for the venture) engraved in rivalry with Wilson and Woollett. "Whether we can in the present day," he writes, "contend with such powerful antagonists as Wilson and Woollett would be at least tried by size, security against risk, and some remuneration for the time of painting. The pictures of ultimate sale I shall be content with; to succeed would perhaps form another epoch in the English school; and if we fall, we fall by contending with giant strength." It is difficult to make out the meaning of even this short extract from this illiterate composition, but it is quite plain that the open rivalry with Wilson, which commenced about 1800, had not ceased in 1822.

But he did not confine his rivalries to English painters, or to the field of landscape art. His long rivalry with Claude commenced with the "Liber Studiorum" in 1807, that with Vandevelde earlier. His famous *Shipwreck* (painted 1805) now in the National Gallery, his perhaps finer *Wreck of the Minotaur*, painted for Lord Yarborough, and his *Fishing Boats in a Squall*, painted for the Marquis of Stafford, and now in the Ellesmere Gallery, besides a fine sea-piece, painted for the Earl of Egremont, are examples of the latter. The Ellesmere picture was painted in direct rivalry with one of Vandevelde's on the same subject, and both hang together in the Ellesmere Gallery. Of them John Burnet wrote:—

"The figures (in the Vandevelde) are made out and coloured without reference to the situation they are in; the sea is beautifully painted, and the foamy tops of the waves blown off by the wind with great observation of nature; nevertheless, the whole work looks little and defined compared with its great competitor. Turner's boat is advancing towards the spectator with all sails set, and a similarity in both pictures is that the sails are prevented from being too cutting and harsh from their melting into and being softened by other sails of a similar shape and colour. A small boat is brought in contact in Turner's, stowing away fish, which forms the principal light, if it may be so called, for there is no strong light in the picture; the lights are of a subdued grey tone even in the yeasty waves; the shape of the mass of light on the water is broad, and of a beautiful form; in Vandervelde's (*sic*) picture it is spotty and devoid of union with the vessel. In Turner we see an obscure outlined form in everything, for though the warm tints of the masses of clouds serve to break down and diffuse the colour of the sails, their form is disturbed by the handling of his brush. In comparing the two pictures as works of art, Vandervelde's must have the preference as far as priority of composition is concerned; but Turner has had the boldness to tell the same story, clothing it with all the grandeur and sublimity of natural representation. The light and shade is very excellent; the mass of dark sky, brought in contact with the sail of the advancing boat, is broad in the extreme."

THE SHIPWRECK.

Of his other rivalries at this period, those with the Poussins and Titian are the most notable. The one produced the famous, and, in spite of its poorness of colour and conventionality, the magnificent, *Goddess of Discord choosing the Apple of Contention in the Garden of Hesperides*, exhibited at the British Institution in 1806, and now in the National Gallery; the other, the *Venus and Adonis*, still more wonderful by reason of the beauty of its colour, its composition, and the audacity of the attempt. This was bought by Mr. Munro of Novar, and was lately sold at Christie's, on the dispersion of the Novar collection, for £1,942. It is, as far as we know, the only picture in which he attempted with success to draw the human form on a large scale, and is certainly one of the best efforts of the English school to rival the "old masters;" the figures, the dogs, and the glorious vine-clad bower in which they are set are all worthy of the subject, and make a picture which reminds one of Titian, Sir Joshua Reynolds, and Etty in about equal proportions.

It is strange that the great sea-pieces we have mentioned were not exhibited (except perhaps that at Petworth), but the occupation of his time by these magnificent works of emulation accounts for his doing so little for the engravers in these years, for they were all probably, except the *Wreck of the Minotaur*, painted before 1807, when he turned his attention to his greatest, and perhaps most successful work of the kind, the "Liber Studiorum." And here we may remark, that emulation with Turner, though it may have been a mark of jealousy, was always a token of respect. Feelings crossed each other in Turner's mind as colours did in his works; it is often difficult to know whether his feeling is to be called noble or base, and the same complexity may be noticed in his "artistic" motives. When imitating other masters he brought his knowledge of nature to bear strongly on his work to make it more natural; when painting a natural scene, he employed all his traditional study to make it more "artistic."

By this time, however, he had learnt nearly all that was to be learnt from art, ancient or modern, in the landscape way, but it was different with nature. That was a book which he could not exhaust, though he was never tired of turning over fresh pages. It was almost his only book, and he began a new chapter about 1801 or 1802, when he made his first tour on the Continent. Previous to this he must have paid a visit to Scotland, for the Exhibition of 1802 contained three Scotch views, one of which was the *Kilchurn* already mentioned. In 1803 he exhibited no less than six foreign subjects, of which one was the *Calais Pier*, now in the National Gallery, another the *Festival upon the opening of the Vintage of Macon*, in the possession of Lord Yarborough; the others were *Bonneville, Savoy, with Mont Blanc*; *Chateaux de Michael, Bonneville, Savoy*; *St. Hugh denouncing vengeance on the Shepherd of Courmayeur in the Valley of d'Aoust*; and *Glacier and Source of the Arvèron going up to the Mer de Glace, in the Valley of the Chamouni*.[22] After this burst of foreign subjects he did not exhibit another scene from abroad for twelve years, except the *Fall of the Rhine at Schaffhausen* (1806), and content this time with simpler, safer, English, a *View of the Castle of St. Michael, near Bonneville, Savoy* (1812). During the next few years the most important picture, and one of the most beautiful he ever painted, was the famous *Sun Rising through vapour: Fishermen cleaning and selling Fish*, exchanged with Sir J. F. Leicester for *The Shipwreck*, and now in the National Gallery, together with *The Shipwreck* and *Spithead: Boat's Crew recovering an Anchor*, another fine picture of the Vandevelde class.

In all these years, during which he kept up this constant rivalry with so many artists, living and dead—and we have not exhausted the list of them—he was continuing his unresting severe study of nature. For many more years this was to continue, this double artistic life, the strife for fame by grand pictures, of which emulation was the motive, the patient development of his knowledge and power by the close study of nature. Few who watched his pictures from year to year could have guessed what a store of beautiful studies of the Alps, about Chamouni, Grenoble, and the Grande Chartreuse he had lying in his portfolios; few could imagine that with materials for landscapes of a truthfulness and an original power never before known, he should prefer to paint pictures in rivalry with the fames of dead men. Possibly he thought that it was the nearest way to fame to show the public that he could beat Vandevelde, Poussin, and the rest of them on their own ground; possibly he may have been diffident of his power to dispense with their aid in composition. However this may have been, he chose to ground his fame so. Even in his "Liber," he in three years gave only three foreign subjects out of twenty plates: *Basle, Mount St. Gothard,* and the *Lake of Thun.*

CHAPTER V.

THE LIBER STUDIORUM—HIS POETRY AND DRAGONS.

IHE 1807 Turner commenced his most serious rivalry, "The Liber Studiorum," a rivalry which not only exceeded in force but differed in quality from his others. Previously he had pitted his skill only against that of the artist rivalled, adopting the style of his rival, but in these engravings he pitted not only his skill, but also his style and range of art against Claude's. There are indeed only a few of the "Liber" prints which are in Claude's style, and most of the best are in his own. Lovely as arc *Woman Playing Tambourine*, and *Hindoo Devotions*, they seem to us far lower in value than *Mount St. Gothard* and *Hind Head Hill*. There is the usual mixture of feeling in the motives with which Turner undertook this work, the same dependence on others for the starting impulse which we see throughout his art-life, the same originality, industry, and confusion of thought in carrying out his design. The idea of the "Liber" did not originate with him, but with his friend Mr. W. F. Wells. The idea was noble in so far as it attempted to extend the bounds of landscape art beyond previous limits, to break down the Claude worship which blinded the eyes of the public to the merit that existed in contemporary work, and prevented them, and artists also, from looking to nature as the source of landscape art.

It is scarcely too much to say that in those days Claude stood between nature and the artist, and that he was as much the standard of landscape art as Pheidias of sculpture. To try to clear away this barrier of progress, as Hogarth had striven years before to abolish the "black masters," was no ignoble effort, and it was done in a nobler spirit than that of Hogarth, for he did not attempt to depreciate his rival. Yet the nobility of the attempt was not unmixed, for if he did not disparage Claude, he attempted to make himself famous at Claude's expense. He did not indeed say, as Hogarth would have done, "Claude is bad, I am good;" but he said, "Claude is good, but I am better." His own experience even from very early days should have told him that, despite the cant of connoisseurs and the strength of old traditions, no purely original work of his had passed unnoticed, and that the truest and noblest way of educating the public taste was by following the bent of his original genius, and leaving the public to draw their own comparisons.

THE DEVIL'S BRIDGE.
From the "Liber Studiorum."

Mr. Wells's daughter states that not only did the "Liber Studiorum" entirely owe its existence to her father's persuasion, but the divisions into "Pastoral," "Elegant Pastoral," "Marine," &c., were also suggested by him. Turner determined to print and publish and sell the "Liber" himself, but to employ an engraver. His first choice fell on "Mr. F. C. Lewis, the best aquatint engraver of the day, who at the very time was at work on facsimiles of Claude's drawings."[23] With him he soon quarrelled. The terms were, that Turner was to etch and Lewis to aquatint at five guineas a plate. The first plate, *Bridge and Goats*, was finished and accepted by Turner, though not published till April, 1812; but the second plate Turner gave Lewis the option of etching as well as aquatinting, and he etched it accordingly, and sent a proof to Turner, raising his charge from five guineas to eight, in consideration of the extra work. Turner praised it, but declined to have the plate engraved, on the ground that Lewis had raised his charges. This ended Mr. Lewis's connection with the "Liber," and Turner next employed Mr. Charles Turner, the mezzotint engraver, but he had to pay him eight guineas a plate. Charles Turner agreed to engrave fifty plates at this price, but after he had finished twenty, he wished to raise his charge to ten guineas, which led to a quarrel. With reference to these quarrels of Turner with his engravers, Mr. Thornbury says, "The painter who had never had quarter given to him when he was struggling, now in his turn, I grieve to say, gave no quarter," and "inflexibly exacting as he was, Turner could not understand how an engraver who had contracted to do fifty engravings should try to get off his bargain at the twenty-first." This, like most of Thornbury's statements, is utterly untrustworthy. There is no evidence to show that a hard bargain was ever driven with him when he was struggling, there is no word of any dispute with engravers till he began to employ them himself, and as to his "not being able to understand" how any man should endeavour to obtain more than the price contracted for, it was exactly what he tried to do himself, when afterwards employed by Cooke.

THE ALPS AT DAYBREAK.
From Rogers's "Poems."

The fact is that in all business arrangements Turner's worse nature, the mean, grasping spirit of the little tradesman, was brought into prominence. In the case of Lewis he was evidently in the wrong, in the case of Charles Turner he was only hard; but in all business transactions he was as a rule ungenerous, and sometimes dishonest. His action towards the public with regard to the "Liber" can be called by no other name. His prices at first were fifteen shillings for prints, and twenty-five shillings for proofs. When the plates got worn (and mezzotint plates are subject to rapid deterioration in the light parts), Turner used to alter them, sometimes changing the effect greatly, as in the *Mer de Glace*, where he transformed the smooth, snow-covered glacier into spiky ridges of ice, or in the *Æsacus* and *Hesperie*, where the effect of sunbeams through the wood was effaced, and the direction in which the head of Hesperie was looking was changed, and the face afterwards concealed. The changes were not always for the worse; the very wear of the plate in some cases, as in that of the *Calm*, improved the effect, and what we have called his confusion of thought, and what Thornbury has called his "distorted logic," may have led him to believe that he was not wrong in selling as he did these worn and altered plates as proofs. A kind casuistry may lend us a word less disagreeable than dishonest to such transactions, but when we know that he habitually from the first made no distinction between proofs and prints—that he sold the same things under different names at different prices—every plea breaks down, and we are forced to the conclusion that when he thought he could cheat safely "the pack of geese,"[24] as he thought the public, he did so.

Nor can we acquit Turner of unfairness in issuing the "Liber Studiorum" in competition with the French painter's "Liber Veritatis," a book well-known to the public and to him, as the third edition of its plates, engraved by Earlom, was just issued, when the "Liber Studiorum" was begun. He must have known what the public did not probably know—that Claude's rough sketches were mere memoranda of the effects of his pictures taken by him to identify them, and never meant for publication; whereas his were carefully-finished compositions, into which he threw his whole power. Not only was the publication unfair as regards Claude, but it was misleading to the public as regards himself. The title, "Liber Studiorum," applies only to some of the prints. A few of the poorer plates, especially the architectural ones, and such simple designs as the *Hedging and Ditching*, might properly perhaps have been called studies, but even upon these he bestowed a care and a finish that would entitle them to be called pictures, monochrome as they are.

The want of a well-considered plan, and the capricious way in which they were published, contributed to the ill-success of the work; and though we are accustomed to look upon its failure as a severe judgment on the taste of the time, we are not at all sure that it would have succeeded if published in the present day, unless Mr. Ruskin had written the advertisement.

"The meaning of the entire book," according to that eloquent writer, "was symbolized in the frontispiece,[25] which he engraved with his own hand:[26] Tyre at Sunset, with the Rape of Europa, indicating the symbolism of the decay of Europe by that of Tyre, its beauty passing away into terror and judgment (Europa being the Mother of Minos and Rhadamanthus)."

Turner's advertisement thus describes the intention of the work:—

"Intended as an illustration of Landscape Composition, classed as follows: Historical, Mountainous, Pastoral, Marine, and Architectural."

We think Turner's description the more correct, and that the intention of his frontispiece was to give all the "classes" in one composition, and we are extremely doubtful whether Turner knew or cared anything about either Minos or Rhadamanthus.

The most obvious intention of the work was to show his own power, and there never was, and perhaps never will be again, such an exhibition of genius in the same direction. No rhetoric can say for it as much as it says for itself in those ninety plates, twenty of which were never published. If he did not exhaust art or nature, he may be fairly said to have exhausted all that was then known of landscape art, and to have gone further than any one else in the interpretation of nature. Notwithstanding, the merit of the plates is very unequal, some, as *Solway Moss* and the *Little Devil's Bridge*, being more valuable as works of art than many of his large pictures; others, especially the architectural subjects, the *Interior of a Church*, and *Pembury Mill*, being almost devoid of interest. As to any one thought running through the series, we can see none, except desire to show the whole range of his power; and as to sentiment, it seems to us to be thoroughly impersonal, impartial, and artistic. He turns on the pastoral or historical stop as easily as if he were playing the organ, and his only concern with his figures is that they shall perform their parts adequately, which is as much as some of them do.

We have spoken of the book as an attack on Claude, and of the "intention" of the work, but we are not sure that we are not using too definite ideas to express the variety of impulses in Turner's mind that tended to the commencement of the "Liber." We have seen that the first notion of it, and its divisions, were suggested by Mr. Wells, and the plates are nothing more nor less than a selection from his sketches and pictures, arranged under these heads. His early topographical drawings and studies in England provided him with the architectural and pastoral subjects, his studies of Claude and the Poussins and Wilson, with the elegant pastoral, Vandevelde and nature with the marine, and his one or two visits to the Continent with the mountainous. The frontispiece, the first attempt to give a coherent signification to the whole, was not published till 1812, and it was not till 1816 that the advertisement to which we have called attention appeared when, after four years' intermission, the issue of the "Liber" was recommenced; even then it is only described as "an illustration of Landscape Composition;" and it is quite probable that the desire to make money, to display his art, to rival Claude, and to educate the public, contributed to the production of the work, without any very vivid consciousness on his part as to his motives of action. It has, like all Turner's work, the characteristics of a gradual growth rather than of the carrying out of a well-defined conception.

FALLS IN VALOMBRÉ.
From Rogers's "Jacqueline."

There is one way in which the title of the book may be considered as appropriate, and that is to take "studia" to mean "studies," in the usual general sense of the word, for it is an index to his whole course of study (including books and excepting colour), down to the time of its publication. With the exception of his Venetian pictures and his later extravagances, it may be said to be an epitome of his art without colour. Poets and painters may change their style, and may develop their powers in after-life in an unexpected manner; but after the age at which Turner had arrived when he commenced to publish the "Liber," viz., thirty-two, there are few, if any, mental germs which have not at least sprouted. Turner, though he never left off acquiring knowledge, or developing his style, is no exception to this rule, and this makes the "Liber" valuable, not only as a collection of works of art, but as a nearly complete summary of the great artist's work and mind. Amongst his more obvious claims to the first place among landscape artists, are his power of rendering atmospherical effects, and the structure and growth of things. He not only knew how a tree looked, but he showed how it grew. Others may have drawn foliage with more habitual fidelity, but none ever drew trunks and branches with such knowledge of their inner life; if you look at the trunks in the drawing of *Hornby Castle* for instance (which we mention because it is easily seen at the South Kensington Museum), and compare them with any others in the same room, the superior indication of texture of bark, of truly varied swelling, of consistency, and all essential differences between living wood and other things, cannot fail to be apparent to the least observant. Although the trees of the "Liber" are not of equal merit (Mr. Ruskin says the firs are not good), this quality may be observed in many of the plates. Others have drawn the appearance of clouds, but Turner knew how they formed. Others have drawn rocks, but he could give their structure, consistency, and quality of surface, with a few deft lines and a wash; others could hide things in a mist, but he could reveal things through mist. Others could make something like a rainbow, but he, almost alone, and without colour, could show it standing out, a bow of light arrested by vapour in mid-air, not flat upon a mountain, or printed on a cloud. If all his power over atmospheric effects and all his knowledge of structure are not contained in the "Liber," there is sufficient proof of them scattered through its plates to do as much justice to them as black and white will allow. If we want to know the result of his studies of architecture we see it here also, little knowledge or care of buildings for their own sakes, but perfect sense of their value pictorially for breaking of lights and casting of shadows; for contrast with the undefined beauty of natural forms, and for masses in composition; for the sentiment that ruins lend, and for the names which they give to pictures. If we seek the books from which his imagination took fire, we have the Bible and Ovid, the first of small, the latter of great and almost solitary power. Jason daring the huge glittering serpent, Syrinx fleeing from Pan, Cephalus and Procris, Æsacus and Hesperie, Glaucus and Scylla, Narcissus and Echo; if we want to know the artists he most admired and imitated, or the places to which he had been, we shall find easily nearly all the former, and sufficient of the latter to show the wide range of his travel. In a word, one who has carefully studied the "Liber" had indeed little to learn of the range and power of Turner's art and mind, except his colour and his fatalism.

The first quotation from the "Fallacies of Hope," nevertheless, was published in the catalogue of 1812, as the motto of his picture of *Snowstorm—Hannibal and his Army Crossing the Alps*, and it is probable that the ill-success of the "Liber" contributed not a little to the gloomy habit of mind which breathes through the fragments of this unfinished composition. These were the lines appended to that grand picture:—

"Craft, treachery, and fraud—Salassian force
Hung on the fainting rear! then Plunder seiz'd
The victor and the captive—Saguntum's spoil,
Alike became their prey; still the chief advanc'd,
Look'd on the sun with hope;—low, broad, and wan.
While the fierce archer of the downward year

Stains Italy's blanch'd barrier with storms.
In vain each pass, ensanguin'd deep with dead,
Or rocky fragments, wide destruction roll'd.
Still on Campania's fertile plains—he thought
But the loud breeze sob'd, Capua's joys beware."

This is nearer to poetry than Turner ever got again. The picture is well-known, and was suggested partly by a storm observed at Farnley, partly by a picture by J. Cozens,[27] of the same subject, from which Turner is reported to have said that he learnt more than from any other.

Turner's love of poetry was shown from the first possible moment. The first pictures to which he appended poetical mottoes were those of 1798, but he could not have used them before, as quotations were never published in the Academy Catalogue prior to that year. When his first original verses were published we cannot tell, but there is little doubt that the lines to his *Apollo and the Python*, in the Catalogue of 1811, were of his own fabrication. They are not from Callimachus, as asserted in the catalogue, but a jumble of the descriptions of two of Ovid's dragons, the Python, and Cadmus's tremendous worm, and are just the peculiar mixture of Ovid, Milton, Thomson, Pope, and the quotations in Royal Academy Catalogues, out of which he formed his poetical style. The Turneresque style of poetry is in fact formed very much in the same way as the Turneresque style of landscape, but the result is not so satisfactory. It required a totally different kind of brain machinery from that which Turner possessed. He may have had a good ear for the music of tones, for he used to play the flute, but he had none for the music of words. Coleridge was an instance of how distinct these two faculties are, as he, whose verses exceed almost all other English verses in beauty of sound, could not tell one note of music from another. Turner lived in a world of light and colour, and beautiful changeful indefinite forms; his thought had visions in place of words; his mind communed with itself in sights and symbols; the procession of his ideas was a panorama. So, where a poet would jot down lines and thoughts, he would print off the impressions on his mental retina; his true poetry was drawn not written—the poetry of instant act, not of laboured thought. How sensible he himself was of the difference, is shown in his clumsy lines:—

"Perception, reasoning, *action's slow ally*,
Thoughts that in the mind awakened lie—
Kindly expand the monumental stone
And as the ... continue power."

This is Mr. Thornbury's reading of part of the longest piece of poetry by Turner yet published, which he has printed without any care, making greater nonsense than even Turner ever wrote, which is saying a great deal. "Awakened" for instance is probably "unwakened," and "monumental stone" is probably "mental store" with another word at the commencement, the word "power" is possibly "pours," as the next line goes on, "a steady current, nor with headlong force," &c. We quite agree with Mr. W. M. Rossetti, that these extracts are not made the best of, though it is doubtful whether the result of more careful editing would be worth the trouble.

There is no picture which better shows the greatness of Turner's power of pictorial imagination than the *Apollo and Python*. We have said that nature was almost Turner's only book. The only written book which there is evidence that he really studied—read through, probably, again and again—is Ovid's "Metamorphoses." That he was fond of poetry there is no doubt, but the sparks that lit his imagination for nearly all his best classical compositions came from this book. This is the only poem which he really *illustrated*, and an edition of Ovid, with engravings from all the scenes which he drew from this source, would make one of the best illustrated books in the world. It would contain *Jason, Narcissus and Echo, Mercury and Herse, Apollo and Python, Apuleia in search of Apuleius* (which is really the story of Appulus, who was turned into a wild olive-tree, Apuleia being a characteristic mistake of Turner's for Apulia. He is sometimes called "a shepherd of Apulia," in notes and translations, and Turner evidently took the name of the country for the name of a woman), *Apollo and the Sibyl, The Vision of Medea, The Golden Bough, Mercury and Argus, Pluto and Proserpine, Glaucus and Scylla, Pan and Syrinx, Ulysses and Polyphemus*. Of all these pictures and designs we have no doubt that, though he referred to other poets in the catalogues and got the idea of some part of the composition from other poets, the original germs are to be found in no other book than Ovid's "Metamorphoses." We have not exhausted the list of his debts to this poet, for it is probable that the first ideas of his Carthage pictures, and all that deal with the history of Æneas, came from the same source, assisted by references to Vergil.

ALLEGORY.
From Rogers's "Voyage of Columbus."

Of all these, excepting the *Ulysses and Polyphemus*, there is none greater than the *Apollo and Python*. Although the figure of Apollo is not satisfactory, it gives an adequate impression of the small size of the boy-god, the radiating glory of his presence, the keen enjoyment of his struggle with the monster, and the triumph of "mind over matter." Of the landscape and the dragon it is difficult to exaggerate the grandeur of the conception; the rocks and trees convulsed with the dying struggles of the gigantic worm, the agony of the brute himself, expressed in the distorted jaws and the twisted tail, the awful dark pool of blood below, the seams in its terrible riven side, studded with a thousand little shafts from Apollo's bow, and the fragments of rock flying in the air above the griffin-like head and noisome steam of breath, make a picture without any rival of its kind in ancient or modern art. It is, as we have said, taken from two dragons of Ovid. Turner seems to have been of the same opinion about books as about nature, and if he wanted anything to complete his picture, went on a few pages and found it. The idea of the god and his bow and arrows is taken from the account of the combat in the first book of the "Metamorphoses," and the idea of the huge dragon with his "poyson-paunch," comes from the same place; but the ruin of the woodland, the flying stones, and the earth blackened with the dragon's gore, come from the description of the combat of Cadmus and his dragon in the third. The larger stone is too huge indeed to be that which Cadmus flung, it has been either, as Mr. Ruskin thinks, lashed into the air by his tail, or, as we think, torn off the rock and vomited into the air; but there is the tree, which the "serpent's weight" did make to bend, and which was "grieved his body of the serpent's tail thus scourged for to be," there is "the stinking breath that goth out from his black and hellish mouth," there is the blood which "did die the green grass black," an idea not in Callimachus nor in Ovid's description of the Python, but which occurs both in the lines appended to the picture and in Ovid's description of Cadmus's serpent. If there were any doubt left as to the influence of this dragon on the picture, there is still another piece of evidence, viz., something very like a javelin, Cadmus's weapon, which is sticking in the dragon, and has reappeared after being painted out, so that it is possible that Turner meant the hero of the picture, in the first instance, to be Cadmus and not Apollo.

The two great dragons of Turner, that which guards the Garden of the Hesperides, and the Python, are specially interesting as the greatest efforts made by Turner's imagination in the creation of living forms, excepting, perhaps, the cloud figure of Polyphemus. They are perhaps the only monsters of the kind created by an artist's fancy, which are credible even for a moment. They will not stand analysis any more than any other painters' monsters, but you can enjoy the pictures without being disturbed by palpable impossibilities. The distance at which we see Ladon helps the illusion; with his fiery eyes and smoking jaws, his spiny back and terrible tail, no one could wish for a more probable reptile. The only objection that has been made to him is that his jaws are too thin and brittle, while Mr. Buskin is extravagant in his praise. It is wonderful to him—

"This anticipation, by Turner, of the grandest reaches of recent inquiry into the form of the dragons of the old earth ... this saurian of Turner's is very nearly an exact counterpart of the model of the iguanodon, now the guardian of the Hesperian Garden of the Crystal Palace, wings only excepted, which are, here, almost accurately, those of the pterodactyle. The instinctive grasp which a healthy imagination takes of *possible* truth, even in its wildest flights, was never more marvellously demonstrated."

Mr. Ruskin then goes on to call attention to—

"The mighty articulations of his body, rolling in great iron waves, a cataract of coiling strength and crashing armour, down amongst the mountain rents. Fancy him moving, and the roaring of the ground under his rings; the grinding down of the rocks by his toothed whorls; the skeleton glacier of him in thunderous march, and the ashes of the hills rising round him like smoke, and encompassing him like a curtain."

The description, fine as it is, seems to us to destroy all belief in Turner's dragon. The wings of a pterodactyle would never lift the body of an iguanodon, and Turner's dragon could not even walk, his comparatively puny body could never even move his miles of tail, let alone lift them. It is far better to leave him where he is; the fact that he is at the top of that rock is sufficient evidence that he got there somehow; how he got there, and how he will get down again, are questions which we had better not ask if we wish to keep our faith in him. Nor can anything be more confused than the notion of a "saurian" with "coiling strength and crashing armour," making the ground "roar under his rings." This might be well enough of a fabulous monster made of iron, but quite inappropriate when applied to a saurian, like the alligator, for instance, with its soft, slow movements, and its bony, skin-padded, noiseless armour.

The Python will stand still less an attempt to define in words what Turner has purposely left mysterious. Not even Mr. Ruskin, we fancy, would dare to pull him out straight from amongst his rocks and trees, and put his griffin's head and talons on to that marvellous body, half worm, half caterpillar. But he is grand, and believable as he is. More simple than either of the other monsters is the single wave of Jason's dragon in his den. This is a mere magnified coil of a simple snake; but its size, its glitter, its incompleteness, the terrible energy of it, its peculiar serpentine wiriness, that elasticity combined with stiffness which is so horrible to see and to feel, make it more awful even than the Python.

We do not believe in Turner's power to evolve even as imperfect a saurian as his Ladon out of his imagination, however "healthy;" and have no doubt that he had seen the fossil remains of an ichthyosaurus. We have the testimony of Mrs. Wheeler that he was much interested in geology,[28] and think it more than probable that the thinness of the monster's jaws and, we may add, the emptiness of his eye socket are due to his drawing them from a fossil, which his knowledge was not great enough to pad with flesh.

CHAPTER VI.

HARLEY STREET, DEVONSHIRE, HAMMERSMITH, AND TWICKENHAM.

1800 TO 1820.

DHE the first ten years of this period we have very little intelligence respecting Turner's life. He moved from Hand Court, Maiden Lane, to 64, Harley Street, in 1799 or 1800, and it is not improbable that he bought the house, as No. 64 and the house next to it in Harley Street, and the house in Queen Anne Street, all belonged to him at the time of his death. There was communication between the three houses at the back, although the corner house fronting both streets did not belong to him. In 1801, 1802, 1803, and 1804, his address in the Royal Academy Catalogue is 75, Norton Street, Portland Road; but in 1804 it is again 64, Harley Street. In 1808[29] it is 64, Harley Street, and West End, Upper Mall, Hammersmith; and this double address is given till 1811, when it is West End, Upper Mall, Hammersmith, only. In and after 1812 it is always Queen Anne Street West, with the addition, from 1814 to 1826, of his house at Twickenham, called Solus Lodge in 1814, and Sandycombe Lodge from 1815 to 1826. It is remarkable that in the Catalogue of the British Institution for 1814 his address is given as Harley Street, Cavendish Square, showing that he had not then given up his house in this street, and this is good evidence that it belonged to him.

The war which broke out with Bonaparte in 1803,[30] and was not finally closed till 1815, prevented him from pursuing his studies of Continental scenery, and he seems during this time to have devoted himself principally to the composition of his great rival pictures, and the "Liber Studiorum," about which we have already written: he stayed occasionally with his friends, Mr. Fawkes at Farnley, where he studied the storm for *Hannibal Crossing the Alps*, and Lord Egremont at Petworth, where he painted *Apuleia and Apuleius*. Almost the only glimpse that we get of his house in Harley Street, though it is very doubtful to what period it belongs, was sent to Mr. Thornbury by Mr. Rose of Jersey:—

"Two ladies, Mrs. R—— and Mrs. H—— once paid him a visit in Harley Street, an extremely rare (in fact, if not the only) occasion of such an occurrence, for it must be known he was not fond of parties prying, as he fancied, into the secrets of his *ménage*. On sending in their names, after having ascertained that he was at home, they were politely requested to walk in, and were shown into a large sitting room without a fire. This was in the depth of winter; and lying about in various places were several cats without tails. In a short time our talented friend made his appearance, asking the ladies if they felt cold. The youngest replied in the negative; her companion, more curious, wished she had stated otherwise, as she hoped they might have been shown into his sanctum or studio. After a little conversation he offered them wine and biscuits, which they partook of for the novelty, such an event being almost unprecedented in his house. One of the ladies bestowing some notice upon the cats, he was induced to remark that he had seven, and that they came from the Isle of Man."[31]

Whatever is the proper date of this story, it is to be feared that he had good reason for not wishing persons to pry into the secrets of his *ménage*. We ourselves have no wish to pry into those secrets; but the fact that Turner had for the greater part of his life a home of which he was ashamed, is sufficient to explain a great deal of his want of hospitality, his churlishness to visitors, and his confirmed habits of secrecy and seclusion.

There is no doubt that he habitually lived with a mistress. Hannah Danby, who entered his service, a girl of sixteen, in the year 1801, and was his housekeeper in Queen Anne Street at his death, is generally considered to have been one; and Sophia Caroline Booth, with whom he spent his last years in an obscure lodging in Chelsea, another. There are many who have lived more immoral lives, and have done more harm to others by their immorality; but he chose a kind of illegal connection which was particularly destructive to himself. He made his home the scene of his irregularities, and, by entering into ultimate relations with uneducated women, cut himself off from healthy social influences which would have given daily employment to his naturally warm heart, and prevented him from growing into a selfish, solitary man. Not to be able to enjoy habitually the society of pure educated women, not to be able to welcome your friend to your hearth, could not have been good for a man's character, or his art, or his intellect.

His uninterrupted privacy possibly enabled him to produce more, and to develop his genius farther in one direction; but we could have well spared many of his pictures for a few works graced with a wider culture and a healthier sentiment. He could paint, and paint, perhaps, better for his isolation—

"The light that never was on sea or land,
The consecration and the Poet's dream."

But it would have been better for him, and, we think, for his art also, if he could have said:—

"Farewell, farewell, the heart that lives alone
Housed in a dream, at distance from the kind!

Such happiness, wherever it be known,
Is to be pitied; for 'tis surely blind."[32]

It was not from any scorn of the conventions of society that he disregarded them, for there is no trace of any feeling of this sort in his pictures or his reported conversations, and in his will he required that the "Poor and Decayed Male Artists," for whom he intended to found a charitable institution ("Turner's Gift"), should be "of *lawful issue*." One reason why he never married may have been his shyness and consciousness of his want of address and personal attraction. Mr. Cyrus Redding, from whom we have one of the brightest and best glimpses of Turner as a man, says:—

"He was aware that he could not hope to gain credit in the world out of his profession. I believe that his own ordinary person was, in his clear-mindedness, somewhat considered in estimating his career in life. He was once at a party where there were several beautiful women. One of them struck him much with her charms and captivating appearance; and he said to a friend, in a moment of unguarded admiration, 'If she would marry me, I would give her a hundred thousand.'"

This, and the increasing absorption in his art of all of himself that could be so absorbed; his desire to economize both his time and his money; his innate hatred of interference with his liberty; his aversion from undertaking any obligation, the consequences of which he could not calculate—all tended to keep him from matrimony, and to make him content with the most unromantic amours.

That he in 1811 or thereabouts could be hospitable and a good companion away from home, is shown by Mr. Redding in his pleasant volume, from which we have just quoted. He met Turner on what appears to have been his first visit to the county to which his family belonged—Devonshire. He met him first, Mr. Redding thinks, at the house of Mr. Collier (the father of Sir Robert Collier), an eminent merchant of Plymouth, and accompanied him on many excursions. On one of these Turner actually gave a picnic "in excellent taste" at a seat on the summit of the hill, overlooking the Sound and Cawsand Bay.

"Cold meats, shell fish, and good wines were provided on that delightful and unrivalled spot. Our host was agreeable, but terse, blunt, and almost epigrammatic at times. Never given to waste his words, nor remarkably choice in their arrangement, they were always in their right place, and admirably effective."[33]

This last sentence sounds somewhat paradoxical, but for that reason is probably all the more accurately descriptive of Turner's art in words. Further on, when defending the great painter, we get a portrait of him as a "plain figure" with "somewhat bandy legs," and "dingy complexion." On another excursion, Redding spent a night at a small country inn with Turner, about three miles from Tavistock, as the artist had a great desire to see the country round at sunrise. The rest of the party, Mr. Collier and two friends, who had spent the day with them on the shores of the Tamar with a scanty supply of provisions, preferred to pass the night at Tavistock.

"Turner was content with bread and cheese and beer, tolerably good, for dinner and supper in one. I contrived to feast somewhat less simply on bacon and eggs, through an afterthought inspiration. In the little sanded room we conversed by the light of an attenuated candle, and some aid from the moon, until nearly midnight, when Turner laid his head upon the table, and was soon sound asleep. I placed two or three chairs in a line, and followed his example at full recumbency. In this way three or four hours' rest were (*sic*) obtained, and we were both fresh enough to go out, as soon as the sun was up, to explore the scenery in the neighbourhood, and get a humble breakfast, before our friends rejoined us from Tavistock. It was in that early morning Turner made a sketch of the picture (*Crossing the Brook*)to which I have alluded, and which he invited me to his gallery to see."

Another of these excursions was to Burr or Borough Island, in Bigbury Bay, "To eat hot lobsters fresh from the sea."

"The morning was squally, and the sea rolled boisterously into the Sound. As we ran out, the sea continued to rise, and off Stake's point became stormy. Our Dutch boat rode bravely over the furrows, which in that low part of the Channel roll grandly in unbroken ridges from the Atlantic."

IVY BRIDGE.
Water-colour in National Gallery.

Two of the party were ill; one, an officer in the army, wanted to throw himself overboard, and they "were obliged to keep him down among the rusty iron ballast, with a spar across him."

"Turner was all the while quiet, watching the troubled scene, and it was not unworthy his notice. The island, the solitary hut upon it, the bay in the bight of which it lay, and the long gloomy Bolt Head to sea-ward, against which the waves broke with fury, seemed to absorb the entire notice of the artist, who scarcely spoke a syllable. While the fish were getting ready, Turner mounted nearly to the highest point of the island rock, *and seemed writing rather than drawing*. The wind was almost too violent for either purpose; what he particularly noted he did not say."

These reminiscences of Mr. Redding contain the most graphic picture of Turner we possess. His carelessness of comfort, his devotion to his art, his power of continuous observation in despite of tumult and discomfort, his love of the sun and the sea, his habit of sketching from a high point of view, his ability to take "pictorial memoranda" in a violent wind, are all striking and essential peculiarities.

It is interesting to learn also from Mr. Redding, that "early in the morning before the rest were up, Turner and myself walked to Dodbrooke, hard by the town, to see the house that had belonged to Dr. Walcot (*sic*), Peter Pindar, and where he was born. Walcot sold it, and there had been a house erected there since; of this the artist took a sketch." Turner probably appreciated Peter's "Advice to Landscape Painters."

One piece of Turner's conversation is also worthy of record, if only on account of its rarity.

"He was looking at a seventy-four gun ship, which lay in the shadow under Saltash. The ship seemed one dark mass.

"'I told you that would be the effect,' said Turner, referring to some previous conversation. 'Now, as you observe, it is all shade.'

"'Yes, I perceive it; and yet the ports are there.'

"'We can only take what is visible—no matter what may be there. There are people in the ship; we don't see them through the planks.'"

This reads like a speech of Dr. Johnson.

We have another account of this same visit to Devonshire from Sir Charles Eastlake, which bears testimony to the hospitality which he received. Miss Pearce, an aunt of Sir Charles, appears to have been his hostess, and her cottage at Calstock the centre of his excursions. A landscape painter, Mr. Ambrose Johns, of great merit, according to Sir Charles, fitted up a small portable painting box, which was of much use to Turner in affording him ready appliances for sketching in oil.

"Turner seemed pleased when the rapidity with which these sketches were done was talked of; for departing from his habitual reserve in the instance of his pencil sketches, he made no difficulty in showing them. On one occasion, when, on his return after a sketching ramble to a country residence belonging to my father, near Plympton, the day's work was shown, he himself remarked that one of the sketches (and perhaps the best) was done in less than half an hour.... On my inquiring what had become of these sketches, Turner replied that they were worthless, in consequence, as he supposed, of some defects in the preparation of the paper; all the grey tints, he observed, had nearly disappeared. Although I did not implicitly rely on that statement, I do not remember to have seen any of them afterwards."[34]

Mr. Johns's devotion was not rewarded till long afterwards, when the great painter sent him a small oil sketch in a letter. Mr. Redding obtained at the time a rough sketch, and these seem to have been the only returns he made for the kindness that was shown to him at Plymouth, though many years afterwards he spoke to Mr. Redding "of the reception he met with on this tour, in a strain that exhibited his possession of a mind not unsusceptible or forgetful of kindness."

The date of this tour is given by Mr. Redding as probably 1811, and by Eastlake 1813 or 1814. The principal pictorial results of it were *Crossing the Brook* (exhibited in 1815), and various drawings for Cooke's *Southern Coast*, which commenced in 1814. It seems probable that his engagement on this work determined his visit to Cornwall and Devonshire, but this is uncertain, as is also whether he paid more than one visit to the locality.

This tour is also interesting from its being the only occasion on which Turner is known to have visited his kinsfolk. We are enabled to state on the authority of one of his family that he went to Barnstaple and called upon his relations there, and a gentleman, late of the Chancery Bar, has kindly supplied us with the following extract of a memorandum made by him in 1853, from facts sworn to in suits instituted to administer Turner's estate.

"Price Turner, an uncle of the painter's, having some idea of educating his son, Thomas Price Turner (now (1853) living at North Street, in the parish of St. Kerrian, Exeter, Professor of Music) as a painter, T. P. T. made, at the request of William Turner, the great artist's father, two drawings as specimens of his ability, one a view of the city of Exeter, taken from the south side, and the other a view of Rougemont Castle, and sent them by Wm. Turner to his son. Shortly after, he (T. P. T.) received a number of water colour drawings, sketches, &c. Some of these were afterwards sent for again, one of which, a water colour view of Redcliffe Church, Bristol, Thomas Price Turner previously copied, which copy, together with the residue of Turner's drawings, are still in his cousin's possession.

"J. M. W. Turner called at Price Turner's house at Exeter about forty years ago (about 1813), and, saying that he called at his father's request, had a conversation with Price Turner and his son and daughter. Thomas Price Turner went to London in 1834 to attend the Royal Musical Festival in commemoration of Handel, in which he was engaged as a chorus singer. He called three times on his cousin, and the third time saw him, but though he (J. M. W. T.) immediately recognized him, the painter gave him a cool reception, never so much as asking him to sit down."

It is probable that Turner's father removed with him to Harley Street in 1800. The powder tax of 1795 is said to have destroyed his trade, and he lived with his son till he died in 1830. He used to strain his son's canvasses and varnish his pictures, "which made Turner say that his father began and finished his pictures for him." As early as 1809, Turner "was in the habit of privately exhibiting such pictures as he did not sell, and the small accumulation he had at Harley Street in 1809 was already dignified with the name of the "Turner Gallery."[35] This gallery Turner's father attended to, showing in visitors &c., and when they stayed at Twickenham he came up to town every morning to open it. Thornbury says that the cost of this weighed upon his spirits until he made friends with a market-gardener, who for a glass of gin a-day, brought him up in his cart on the top of the vegetables. This is said to have been after Turner removed from Harley Street, and was very well off if not rich, for he had built his house in Queen Anne Street and his lodge at Twickenham,[36] both of which belonged to him, as well as the land at Twickenham, and (probably) the house in Harley Street. Turner's father made great exertions to add to his son's estate at Sandycombe, by running out little earthworks in the road and then fencing them round. At one time there was a regular row of these fortifications, which used to be called "Turner's Cribs." One day, however, they were ruthlessly swept away by some local authority. If, however, both father and son were very "saving" and eccentric in their ways, they were devoted to one another from the beginning to the end, to an extent very touching and beautiful, however strange in its manifestation.

Of Turner's life at West End, Upper Mall, Hammersmith, we have only the following glimpse in a communication to Thornbury by "a friend."

"The garden, which ran down to the river, terminated in a summer-house; and here, out in the open air, were painted some of his best pictures. It was there that my father, who then resided at Kew, became first acquainted with him; and expressing his surprise that Turner could paint under such circumstances, he remarked that lights and room were absurdities, and that a picture could be painted anywhere. His eyes were remarkably strong. He would throw down his water-colour drawings on the floor of the summer-house, requesting my father not to touch them, as he could see them there, and they would be drying at the same time."

It may have been when at Hammersmith that he became acquainted with Mr. Trimmer, for in a letter to Mr. Wyatt of Oxford respecting two pictures of that city, which is dated "West End, Upper Mall, Hammersmith, Feb. 4, 1810," he says, "Pray tell me likewise of a gentleman of the name of Trimmer, who has written to you to be a subscriber for the print." This gentleman was the Rev. Henry Scott Trimmer, Vicar of Heston, who was one of Turner's best and most intimate friends till his death. It is said that he first went to Hammersmith to be near De Loutherbourg, and it is probable that one of his reasons for building on his free—hold at Twickenham was to be nearer Mr. Trimmer. De Loutherbourg died in 1812.

Sandycombe Lodge, first called Solus Lodge, is on the road from Twickenham to Isleworth, and is built on low lying ground and damp. The original structure has been added to, but the additions being built of brick, it is easy to see how it looked in Turner's time—a small semi-Italian villa covered with plaster and decorated with iron balustrades and steps. It is within walking distance (4 miles) of Heston. We are able by the kindness of Mr. F. E. Trimmer, the youngest son of Turner's friend, to correct some false impressions conveyed by Thornbury's garbled account of what he was told by the eldest son.

The Rev. Henry Scott Trimmer, the son of the celebrated Mrs. Trimmer, and father of the Rev. Henry Syer Trimmer, who gave Thornbury his information, was about the same age as Turner, and very much interested in art. As an amateur painter he attained considerable skill, having a wonderful faculty for catching the manner of other artists. His great knowledge of pictures, and his continual experiments in the way of mediums, colours, and devices for obtaining effects, made his acquaintance specially interesting and valuable to Turner, and Turner's to him. No better proof of his ability can be found than the two following stories:—

There is a picture at Heston before which Turner would frequently stand studying. It is a sea-piece with the sun behind a mist, and with a golden hazy effect not unlike Turner's famous *Sun rising in a Mist*, but the sea washes up to the frame. One day Turner said to Mr. Trimmer, "I like that picture; there's a good deal in it. Where did you get it?" (Or words to this effect.) "I painted it," was the reply; upon which the artist turned away without a word, and never looked at the picture again.

The true story of the picture, supposed to be by Sir Joshua Reynolds, to which Mr. Trimmer added a background, is this.[37] He purchased it in an unfinished condition of a dealer in Holborn, and finished it himself, and it remained in his possession till his death, when his son (Mr. F. E. Trimmer), knowing its history, kept it out of the sale at Christie's of his father's fine collection, and sold it, among other less valuable and genuine productions, at Heston. The dealer who bought it (for £6) thought he had made a great catch, and inquired of Mr. Trimmer's son the history of the picture, which he considered a splendid Sir Joshua, speaking especially of the background as being a proof of its authenticity. When Mr. Trimmer told him that his father had bought it in his own shop and had finished it himself, he would not believe it for a long time.

Of the other stories of Turner's connection with Heston, and of his power to assist others in the composition of their pictures, the following is perhaps the most interesting:—[38]

Once when Howard (R.A.) was staying at the vicarage, painting a portrait of Mr. Trimmer's second son, the Rev. Barrington James Trimmer, Turner was always finding fault with the work in progress. It was a full-size and full-length portrait of a boy of three years old, dressed in a white frock and red morocco shoes. One day Howard, annoyed at Turner's frequent objections, told him that he had better do it himself, on which Turner said, "This is what I should do," and taking up the cat he wrapped its body in his red pocket handkerchief, and put it under the boy's arm. The effect of this, as may still be seen in the picture at the house of Mr. Trimmer's son at Heston, was excellent. The cat gave an interest to the figure which it wanted, the red morocco shoes were no longer isolated patches of bright colour at the bottom of the picture, the blank expanse of white frock was varied and lightened up by the red handkerchief and pussy's tabby face, and the work, which was on the brink of failure, was a decided success. Parts of the cat, handkerchief, and landscape were put in by Turner.

Sketching with oils on a large canvas in a boat, driving out on little sketching excursions in his gig with his ill-tempered nag Crop Ear, said to have been immortalized in his picture of the *Frosty Morning* (which was, however, painted before he went to Twickenham), fishing for trout in the Old Brent, or for roach in the Thames, with Mr. Trimmer's sons, digging his pond in his garden and planting it round with weeping willows and alders, the picture of Turner's life at Twickenham is a pleasant and healthy one. At Heston he drew his *Interior of a Church* for the "Liber," and actually gave away two of his drawings to Mrs. Trimmer, one of a Gainsborough, which they had seen together on an excursion to Osterley House, and one of a woman gathering watercresses, whom they had met on their way. But these gifts were asked for by the lady, and Turner would not let them go without making *replicas*. He once stood with a long rod two whole days in a pouring rain under an umbrella fishing in a small pond in the vicarage garden, without even a nibble.

In connection with the Trimmers we get other instances of his rare and bare hospitality, which showed that he never altered his manner of living after he left Maiden Lane. We must refer the reader to Mr. Thornbury's life for the remainder of these varied, interesting, and on the whole pleasant reminiscences.

Space, however, we must spare for a letter, very incorrectly given by Thornbury, the only record of his second attachment, the object of which was the sister of the Rev. H. Scott Trimmer, who was at that time being courted by her future husband:—

"Tuesday. Aug. 1. 1815.
"QUEEN ANNE ST.

"MY DEAR SIR,

"I lament that all hope of the pleasure of seeing you or getting to Heston—must for the present wholly vanish. My father told me on Saturday last when I was as usual compelled to return to town the same day, that you and Mrs. Trimmer would leave Heston for Suffolk as tomorrow Wednesday, in the first place, I am glad to hear that her health is so far established as to be equal to the journey, and believe me your utmost hope, for her benefitting by the sea air being fully realized will give me great pleasure to hear, and the earlier the better.

"After next Tuesday—if you have a moments time to spare, a line will reach me at Farnley Hall, near Otley Yorkshire, and for some time, as Mr. Fawkes talks of keeping me in the north by a trip to the Lakes &c. until November therefore I suspect I am not to see Sandycombe. Sandycombe sounds just now in my ears as an act of folly, when I reflect how little I have been able to be there this year, and less chance (perhaps) for the next in looking forward to a Continental excursion, & poor Daddy seems as much plagued with weeds as I am with disapointments, that if Miss —— would but wave bashfulness, or—in other words—make an offer instead of expecting one—the same might change occupiers—but not to teaze you further, allow with most sincere respects to Mrs. Trimmer and family, to consider myself

"Your most truly (or sincerely) obliged
"J. M. TURNER."

But for the assurance of the present Mr. Trimmer, of Heston, that this attachment of Turner to Miss Trimmer was undoubted, and that this letter has always been considered in the family as a declaration thereof, we should have thought that the offer he wanted was one for Sandycombe Lodge and not for his hand. It is, however, past doubt that Turner was violently smitten, and though forty years old, felt it much.

The above letter was the only one known to have been written by Turner to his friend the Vicar of Heston, and it is quite untrue, as asserted by Thornbury, that the Vicar's letters were burnt in sackfuls by his son. His large correspondence was patiently gone through—a task which took some years. Thornbury was probably thinking of the destruction of the celebrated Mrs. Trimmer's correspondence by her daughter, in which it is true that sackfuls of interesting letters perished.

CHAPTER VII.

ITALY AND FRANCE.

1820 TO 1840.

THE life of Turner the man, that is, what we know of it, during these twenty years, may be written almost in a page—the history of his art might be made to fill many volumes. During this period he exhibited nearly eighty pictures at the Royal Academy, and about five hundred engravings were published from his drawings. If he had been famous before, he was something else, if not something more than famous now; he was "the fashion." It was on this ground that Sir Walter Scott, who would have preferred Thomson of Duddingstone to illustrate his 'Provincial Antiquities' (published in 1826), agreed to the employment of Turner, who afterwards (in 1834) furnished a beautiful series of sixty-five vignettes for Cadell's edition of Sir Walter's prose and poetical works.

In 1819 Turner paid his first visit to Italy, which had a marked influence on his style. From this time forward his works become remarkable for their colour. Down to this time he had painted principally in browns, blues, and greys, employing red and yellow very sparingly, but he had been gradually warming his scale almost from the beginning. From the wash of sepia and Prussian blue, he had slowly proceeded in the direction of golden and reddish brown, and had produced both drawings and pictures with wonderful effects of mist and sunlight, but he had scarcely gone beyond the sober colouring of Vandevelde and Ruysdael till he began his great pictures in rivalry with Claude. In them may be seen perhaps the dawn of the new power in his art. In the Exhibition of 1815 were two prophecies of his new style, in which he was to transcend all former efforts in the painting of distance and in colour. These were *Crossing the Brook*, with its magical distance, and *Dido building Carthage*, with its blazing sky and brilliant feathery clouds. The first is the purest and most beautiful of all his oil pictures of the loveliness of English scenery, the most simple in its motive, the most tranquil in its sentiment, the perfect expression of his enjoyment of the exquisite scenery in the neighbourhood of Plymouth. The latter with all its faults was the finest of the kind he ever painted, and his greatest effect in the way of colour before his visit to Italy. In his other Carthage picture of this period, *The Decline* (exhibited 1817), the "brown demon," as Mr. Ruskin calls it, was in full force, and his pictures of *Dido and Æneas* (1814), *The Temple of Jupiter* (1817), and *Apuleia and Apuleius*, are cold and heavy in comparison. Indeed, from 1815 to 1823 his power, judged by his exhibited pictures, seemed to be flagging.

Whether his second disappointment in love had anything to do with this we have no means of judging, but if it disturbed for a time his power of painting for fame, it certainly had no ill effect either as to the quantity or quality of his water-colours for the engravers.

His most worthy and beautiful work of these years is to be found not in his oil pictures but in his drawings for Dr. Whitaker's 'History of Richmondshire' (published 1823) and the 'Rivers of England' (1824). Both series were engraved in line in a manner worthy of the artist. One of the former, the *Hornby Castle*, a little faded perhaps, but still exquisite in its harmonies of blue and amber, is to be seen at South Kensington. Three more were lately exhibited by Mr. Ruskin—*Heysham Village*, *Egglestone Abbey*, and *Richmond*. Of this series Mr. Ruskin says, "The foliage is rich and marvellous in composition, the effects of mist more varied and true" (than in the *Hakewill* drawings), "the rock and hill drawing insuperable, the skies exquisite in complex form." The engravings probably owed much to Turner's own supervision, and many of them, such as *Egglestone Abbey*, by T. Higham, and *Wycliffe*, by John Pye, Middiman's *Moss Dale Fall*, and Radcliffe's *Hornby Castle*, were perfect translations of the originals, showing an advance in the art of engraving as great as that which Turner had made in water-colour drawing. Except in the heightened scale of colour there is little in this series to show the influence of Italy, their temper is that of *Crossing the Brook*, and the foliage and scenery that of England. Nor do we find anything but England in the 'Rivers.' Nothing can be more purely English than the exquisite drawing of *Totnes on the Dart* (of which we give a woodcut). The original is one of the treasures of the National Gallery, and is marvellous for the minuteness of its finish and the breadth and truth of its effect. The tiny group of poplars in the middle distance are painted with such dexterity that the impression of multitudinous leafage is perfectly conveyed, and the stillness of clear smooth water filled with innumerable variegated reflections, the beautiful distance with castle, church, and town, and the group of gulls in the foreground, make a picture of placid beauty in which there is no straining for effect, no mannerism, nothing to remind you of the artist. It is only in the touches of red in the fore of the river (touches unaccounted for by anything in the drawing) that you discern him at last, and find that you are looking not at nature but "a Turner." If you are inclined to be angry with these touches, cover them with the hand and find out how much of the charm is lost.

TOTNES ON THE DART.
From "Rivers of England."

After the 'Rivers of England,' Turner produced work more magnificent in colour, more transcendent in imagination, indeed *the* work which singles him out individually from all landscape artists, in which the essences of the material world were revealed in a manner which was not only unrealized but unconceived before; but for perfect balance of power, for the mirroring of nature as it appears to ninety-nine out of every hundred, for fidelity of colour of both sky and earth, and form (especially of trees), for carefulness and accuracy of drawing, for work that neither startles you by its eccentricity nor puzzles you as to its meaning, which satisfies without cloying, and leaves no doubt as to the truth of its illusion, there is none to compare with these drawings of his of England after his first visit to Italy—and especially (though perhaps it is because we know them best that we say so) the drawings for the 'Rivers of England.' We are certain at least of this, that no one has a right to form an opinion about Turner's power generally, either to go into ecstasies over or to deride his later work, till he has seen some of these matchless drawings. They form the true centre of his artistic life, the point at which his desire for the simple truth and the imperious demands of his imagination were most nearly balanced.

In 1821 and 1824 Turner exhibited no pictures at the Royal Academy, and it would have been no loss to his fame if his pictures of 1820 and 1822, *Rome, from the Vatican*, and *What you will*, had never left his studio; but in 1823 he astonished the world with the first of those magnificent dreams of landscape loveliness with which his name will always be specially associated;—*The Say of Baiæ with Apollo and the Sibyl* (1823). The three supreme works of this class,

The Bay of Baiæ, Caligula's Palace and Bridge (1831), and *Childe Harold's Pilgrimage* (1832), are too well known to need description, and have been too much written about to need much comment. They were the realization of his impressions of Italy, with its sunny skies, its stone-pines, its ruins, its luxuriance of vegetation, its heritage of romance. How little the names given to these pictures really influence their effect, is shown by the frequency with which one of them is confused with another. What verses of what poet, what episode of history may have been in the artist's mind is of little consequence, when the thought is expressed in the same terms of infinite sunny distance, crumbling ruin and towering tree. The artist may have meant to embody the whole of Byron's mind in the *Childe Harold*, the history of Italy in *Caligula's Palace and Bridge*, the folly of life in *Apollo and the Sibyl*, but it does not matter now, the things are "Turners," neither more nor less; we doubt very much whether Turner cared greatly for the particular stories attached to many of his pictures. Some of them remind us of a title of a picture in the Academy of 1808, *A Temple and Portico, with the drowning of Aristobulus, vide Josephus, book 15, chap. 3*. In some it was no doubt his ardent desire to proclaim his thoughts on history and fate, but the result is much the same, for the medium in which he attempted to convey them was that least suited for his purpose. It was, however, his only means of expression, and there is something very sad in the idea of a mind struggling in vain to give its most serious thoughts didactic force. If these thoughts had been profound, and the mind that of a prophet, the failure would have been tragical. The language employed was the highest of its kind, but it was as inadequate for its purpose as music. It has, however, like fine music, the power of starting vibrations of sentiment full of suggestion, giving birth to endless dreams of beauty and pleasure, of sadness and foreboding, according to the personality and humour of those who are sensitive to its charm.

In 1825 were published his first illustrations to a modern poet—Byron; he contributed some more to the editions of 1833 and 1834, most of them being views of places which he had never seen, and therefore compositions from the sketches of others, like his drawings for Hakewill's "Picturesque Tour of Italy" and Finden's "Illustrations of the Bible." No doubt the experience of his youth in improving the sketches of amateurs and the liberty which such work gave to his imagination, made it easy and congenial to him. These drawings show the variety of his artistic power and the perfection of his technical skill. The *Hakewill* series is marvellous for minute accuracy (being taken from camera sketches) and for beautiful tree drawing, and the Bible series for imagination. They are, however, of less interest in a biography than those which were based upon his own impressions of the scenes depicted, such as his illustrations to Rogers and Scott.

In 1825 he exhibited only one picture, *Harbour of Dieppe*, and in 1826, the year when the publication of the "Southern Coast" terminated, three, of one of which there is told a story of unselfish generosity, which deserves special record. The picture was called *Cologne—the arrival of a Packet-boat—Evening*. Of this Mr. Hamerton writes: "There were such unity and serenity in the work, and such a glow of light and colour, that it seemed like a window opened upon the land of the ideal, where the harmonies of things are more perfect than they have ever been in the common world." The picture was hung between two of Sir Thomas Lawrence's portraits, and Turner covered its glowing glory with a wash of lampblack, so as not to spoil their effect. "Poor Lawrence was so unhappy," he said. "It will all wash off after the Exhibition." As Mr. Hamerton truly observes, "It is not as if Turner had been indifferent to fame."

There are many stories of apparently contrary action on Turner's part, namely, of heightening the colour of his pictures to "kill" those of his neighbours at the Academy, but they do not spoil this story. During those merry "varnishing days" which Turner enjoyed so much, attempts to outcolour one another were ordinary jokes—give-and-take sallies of skill, made in good humour. No one entered into such contests with more zest than Turner, and he was not always the victor. This story seems to us to prove that when Turner saw that any one was really hurt, his tenderness was greater than his spirit of emulation and jest.

Leslie tells the best of the "counter stories."

"In 1832, when Constable exhibited his *Opening of Waterloo Bridge*,[39] it was placed in the School of Painting—one of the small rooms at Somerset House.

A sea piece,[40] by Turner, was next to it—a grey picture, beautiful and true, but with no positive colour in any part of it—Constable's *Waterloo* seemed as if painted with liquid gold and silver, and Turner came several times into the room while he was heightening with vermilion and lake the decorations and flags of the City barges. Turner stood behind him, looking from the *Waterloo* to his own picture, and at last brought his palette from the great room, where he was touching another picture, and putting a round daub of red lead, somewhat bigger than a shilling, on his grey sea, went away without saying a word. The intensity of the red lead, made more vivid by the coolness of the picture, caused even the vermilion and lake of Constable to look weak. I came into the room just as Turner left it. 'He has been here,' said Constable, 'and fired a gun.'"

On the opposite wall was a picture, by Jones, of Shadrach, Meshach, and Abednego in the furnace.[41] "A coal," said Cooper, "has bounced across the room from Jones's picture, and set fire to Turner's sea." The great man did not come into the room for a day and a half; and then in the last moments that were allowed for painting, he glazed the scarlet seal he had put on his picture, and shaped it into a buoy."[42]

This daub of red lead was rather defensive than offensive, and there is no story of Turner which shows any malice in his nature. To his brother artists he was always friendly and just; he never spoke in their disparagement, and often helped young artists with a kind word or a practical suggestion. Even Constable—between whom and Turner not much love was lost, according to Thornbury—he helped on one occasion by striking in a ripple in the foreground of his picture—the "something" just wanted to make the composition satisfactory. We think, then, that we may enjoy the beautiful story of self-sacrifice for Lawrence's sake, without any disagreeable reflection that it is spoilt by others showing a contrary spirit towards his brother artists.

The year 1826 was his last at Sandycombe. As he had taken it for the sake of his father, so he gave it up, for "Dad" was always working in the garden and catching cold. He took this step much to his own sorrow, we believe, and much to our and his loss. Without the pleasant and wholesome neighbourhood of the Trimmers, with no home but the gloomy, dirty, disreputable Queen Anne Street, he became more solitary, more self-absorbed, or absorbed in his art (much the same thing with him), and lived only to follow unrestrained wherever his wayward genius led him, and to amass money for which he could find no use. How he still loved to grasp it, however, and how unscrupulous he was in doing so, is painfully shown in his dispute with Cooke about this time (1827), which prevented a proposed continuation of the "Southern Coast." Mr. Cooke's letter relating to it, though long, is too important to omit, and, though it may be said to be *ex parte*, carries sad conviction of its truth:—

"*January 1, 1827.*

"DEAR SIR,

"I cannot help regretting that you persist in demanding twenty-five sets of India proofs before the letters of the continuation of the work of the 'Coast,' besides being paid for the drawings. It is like a film before your eyes, to prevent your obtaining upwards of two thousand pounds in a commission for drawings for that work.

"Upon mature reflection you must see I have done all in my power to satisfy you of the total impossibility of acquiescing in such a demand; it would be unjust both to my subscribers and to myself.

"The 'Coast' being my own original plan, which cost me some anxiety before I could bring it to maturity, and an immense expense before I applied to you, when I gave a commission for drawings to upwards of £400, *at my own entire risk*, in which the shareholders were not willing to take any part, I did all I could to persuade you to have one share, and which I did from a firm conviction that it would afford some remuneration for your exertions on the drawings, in addition to the amount of the contract. The share was, as it were, forced upon you by myself, with the best feelings in the world; and was, as you well know, repeatedly refused, under the idea that there was a possibility of losing money by it. You cannot deny the result: a constant dividend of profit has been made to you at various times, and will be so for some time to come.

"On Saturday last, to my utter astonishment, you declared in my print-rooms, before three persons, who distinctly heard it, as follows: 'I will have my terms, or I will oppose the work by doing another "Coast!"' These were the words you used, and every one must allow them to be a *threat*.

"And this morning (Monday), you show me a note of my own handwriting, with these words (or words to this immediate effect): 'The drawings for the future "Coast" shall be paid twelve guineas and a half each.'

"Now, in the name of common honesty, how can you apply the above note to any drawings for the first division of the work called the 'Southern Coast,' and tell me I owe you two guineas on each of those drawings? Did you not agree to make the whole of the 'South Coast' drawings at £7 10*s.* each? and did I not continue to pay you that sum for the first four numbers? When a meeting of the partners took place, to take into consideration the great exertions that myself and my brother had made on the plates, to testify their entire satisfaction, and considering the difficulties I had placed myself in by such an agreement as I had made (dictated by my enthusiasm for the welfare of a work which had been planned and executed with so much zeal, and of my being paid the small sum only of twenty-five guineas for each plate, including the loan of the drawings, for which I received no return or consideration whatever on the part of the shareholders), they unanimously (excepting on your part) and very liberally increased the price of each plate to £40; and I agreed, on my part, to pay you ten guineas for each drawing after the fourth number. And have I not kept this agreement? Yes; you have received from me, and from Messrs. Arch on my account, the whole sum so agreed upon, and for which you have given me and them receipts. The work has now been finished upwards of six months, when you show me a note of my own handwriting, and which was written to you in reply to a part of your letter, where you say, 'Do you imagine I shall go to John O'Groat's House for the same sum I receive for the Southern part?' Is this *fair* conduct between man and man—to apply the note (so explicit in itself) to the former work, and to endeavour to make me believe I still owe you two guineas and a-half on each drawing? Why, let me ask you, should I promise you such a sum? What possible motive could I have in heaping gold into your pockets, when you have always taken such especial care of your interests, even in the case of *Neptune's Trident*, which I can declare you *presented* to me; and, in the spirit of *this* understanding, I presented it again to Mrs. Cooke. You may recollect afterwards charging me two guineas for the loan of it, and requesting me at the same time to return it to you, which has been done.

"The ungracious remarks I experienced this morning at your house, where I pointed out to you the meaning of my former note—that it referred to the future part of the work, and not to the 'Southern Coast'—were such as to convince me that you maintain a mistaken and most unaccountable idea of profit and advantage in the new work of the 'Coast,' and that no estimate or calculation will convince you to the contrary.

"Ask yourself if Hakewill's 'Italy,' 'Scottish Scenery,' or 'Yorkshire' works have either of them succeeded in the return of the capital laid out on them.

"These works have had in them as much of your individual talent as the 'Southern Coast,' being modelled on the principle of it; and although they have answered your purpose, by the commissions for drawings, yet there is considerable doubt remaining whether the shareholders and proprietors will ever be reinstated in the money laid out on them. So much for the profit of works. I assure you I must turn over an entirely new leaf to make them ever return their expenses.

"To conclude, I regret exceedingly the time I have bestowed in endeavouring to convince you in a calm and patient manner of a number of calculations made for *your* satisfaction; and I have met in return such hostile treatment that I am positively disgusted at the mere thought of the trouble I have given myself on such a useless occasion.

> "I remain,
> "Your obedient servant,
> "W. B. COOKE."

When we realize that this was the same man that closed his connection with Mr. Lewis, because he would not both etch and aquatint the plates of the Liber for the same terms as those agreed upon for aquatinting alone, we are able to understand why he was characterized as a "great Jew," in a letter of introduction, which he brought from a publisher in London to one in Yorkshire, when he went to that county to illustrate Dr. Whitaker's *History of Richmondshire*. Mrs. Whitaker, who was his hostess at the time, hearing of this took the phrase literally, and, says Mr. Hamerton, "treated him as an Israelite indeed, possibly with reference to church attendance and the consumption of ham."

In 1827 was published the first part of his largest series of prints, the "England and Wales," which were engraved with matchless skill by that trained band of engravers who brought, with the artist's assistance, the art of engraving landscapes in line to a point never before attained. The history of Turner and his engravers has yet to be fully written; the number of them from first to last is extraordinary, probably nearly one hundred. Of these, twenty, and nearly all the best, were employed on this work—Goodall, Wallis, Willmore, W. Miller, Brandard, Radcliffe, Jeavons, W. R. Smith, and others. Never before was so great an artist surrounded by such a skilled body of interpreters in black and white. The drawings were unequal in merit, but nearly all of them wonderful for power of colour and daring effect, with ever lessening regard for local accuracy. The artist threw aside all traditions and conventions, and proclaimed himself as "Turner," the great composer of chromatic harmonies in forms of sea and sky, hills and plains, sunshine and storm, towns and shipping, castles and cathedrals. He could not do this without sacrificing much of truth, and much of what was essential truth in a work whose aim was professedly topographical. Imaginative art of all kinds has a code analogous to, but not identical with, the moral code: beauty takes the seat of virtue and harmony of truth, and when the work is purely imaginative, there is no conflict between fancy and fact which can make the strictest shake his head. But when known facts are dealt with by the imagination, the conflict arises immediately, and it would scarcely be possible to find a case in which it was more obvious than in Turner's "England and Wales," in which he made the familiar scenes of his own country conform to the authoritative conception of his pictorial fancy. Whether he was right or wrong in raising the cliffs of England to Alpine dignity, in saturating her verdant fields with yellow sun, in exaggerating this, in ignoring that, has been argued often, and will be argued over and over again; but all art is a compromise, and the precise justice of the compromise will ever be a matter of opinion. Art *v.* Nature is a cause which will last longer than any Chancery suit. Even artists cannot agree as to the amount of licence which it is proper to take, but they are all conscious that they at least keep on the right side; one thing only, all, or nearly all, are agreed upon, and that is that licence must be taken, or art becomes handicraft. About Turner almost the only thing which can be said with certainty is that he stretched his liberty to the extreme limits.

Yet to the pictorial code of morals he was the most faithful of artists, he almost always reached beauty, his harmonies were almost always perfect, and he strove after his own peculiar generalization of fact, and his own peculiar extract of truth with the greatest ardour. This extract was his impression of a place, made up generally (at least in his foreign scenes) of two or three sketches taken from different points of view, and he was very careful to study not only the principal features of the country, but the costume and employment of the inhabitants, and the description of local vehicle, on wheels or keel. From these studies would arise the conception of one scene, combining all that his mind retained as essential—a growth which, however false it might appear when compared with the actual facts of the place from one point of view, contained nothing but what had a germ of truth, and of local truth. That this applies to all his drawings we do not say, but we are confident that it does to most. Many of his drawings for the "England and Wales" were probably taken from sketches that had lain in his portfolios for years, and were dressed up by him when wanted, with such accessories of storm and rainbow as occurred to his fancy, or to his memory and feelings as connected with the spot. There is, we think, no doubt that Turner strove to be conscientious; but his conscience was a "pictorial" conscience, and no man can judge him. We can only take his works as they are, and be thankful that all the strange confusions of his mind, and mingled accidents of his life, have produced so unique and beautiful a result as the "England and Wales." It is no use now regretting that his vast powers in their prime were used wastefully in what will appear to many as the falsification of English landscape; it is far better to rejoice that the genius and knowledge of the man were so transcendent that, in spite of all the worst that can be said, each separate drawing is precious in itself as a record of natural phenomena, and a masterly arrangement of indefinite forms and beautiful colour.

Mr. Ruskin affirms that, "howsoever it came to pass, a strange, and in many respects grievous metamorphosis takes place upon him about the year 1825. Thenceforth he shows clearly the sense of a terrific wrongness, and sadness, mingled in the beautiful order of the earth; his work becomes partly satirical, partly reckless, partly—and in its greatest and noblest features—tragic." We are not prepared to assent to this entirely, especially as Mr. Ruskin states immediately afterwards that one at least of the manifestations of "this new phase of temper" can be traced unmistakably in the "Liber," which was concluded six years before; but there is no doubt that his work for some of these years was distinguished by recklessness and caprice in an unusual degree, and we have little doubt that his removal from Sandycombe, and the consequent loss of healthy companionship, had something to do with it. During three years he exhibited no pictures of special interest, except the *Cologne* of 1826, and the *Ulysses deriding Polyphemus* of 1829. This latter picture we take to be a sure sign of recovery, as it shows perhaps the most complete balance of power of any of his large works, being not less wonderful for happy choice of subject than for grandeur of conception and splendour of colour—the first picture in which, since the *Apollo and Python* of 1811, the union between the literary subject and the landscape, or (if we must use that horrid word) seascape, was perfect. This picture was no *Temple and Portico, with the drowning of Aristobulus.* The grand indefinite figure of the agonized giant, the crowded ship of Ulysses, the water-nymphs and the dying sun, are all parts of one conception, and show what Turner could do when his imagination was thoroughly inflamed. Whence the inspiration was derived it is difficult to say. Like most of his inspirations, it probably had more than one source. Homer's Odyssey is the source given in the catalogue; but it is probable, as we before have hinted, that the figure of Polyphemus was suggested by the splendid description in the fourteenth book of Ovid's Metamorphoses. Many years had lapsed since he had shown the full force of his imagination under the influence of classical story, and he was never to do so again. Subjects of the kind suited to his peculiar genius were difficult to find, and he had no such habitual intercourse with his intellectual peers as enabled him to gather suggestions for his works. He was thrown entirely on his own uneducated resources, and the result was, with his imperfect knowledge of his own strength and the limits of his art, partial failure of most, and total failure of many of his most strenuous efforts. This is one of the saddest facts of his art-life, the frequent waste, or partial waste, of unique power.

His increasing isolation of mind was mitigated no doubt by constant visits to Petworth, Farnley, and other houses of his friends and patrons, by the chaff of "varnishing days," by social meetings of the Academy Club, and by frequent travel; but it increased notwithstanding. Not Mr. Trimmer, nor Lord Egremont, nor even his friends and fellow Academicians, Chantrey and Jones, could break through his barrier of reserve and see the man Turner face to face. From the beginning he had his secrets, and he kept them to the end. He could be merry and social in a gathering where the talk never became confidential, and with children (whom he could not distrust); but his living-rooms in Queen Anne Street, his painting-room wherever he was, and his heart, were, with scarcely an exception, opened to none. At Petworth, Lord

Egremont indeed was allowed to enter his studio; but he had to give a peculiar knock agreed upon between them before he would open the door.

In 1828 he was at Rome again, from which place he wrote the following letters[43] to Chantrey and Jones of unusual length and interest.

"TO GEORGE JONES, R.A.

"ROME,
"*Oct. 13, 1828.*

"DEAR JONES,

"Two months nearly in getting to this terra pictura, *and at work*; but the length of time is my own fault. I must see the South of France, which almost knocked me up, the heat was so intense, particularly at Nismes and Avignon; and until I got a plunge into the sea at Marseilles, I felt so weak that nothing but the change of scene kept me onwards to my distant point. Genoa, and all the sea-coast from Nice to Spezzia, is remarkably rugged and fine; so is Massa. Tell that fat fellow Chantrey that I did think of him, *then* (but not the first or the last time) of the thousands he had made out of those marble craigs which only afforded me a sour bottle of wine and a sketch; but he deserves everything which is good, though he did give me a fit of the spleen at Carrara.

"Sorry to hear your friend, Sir Henry Bunbury, has lost his lady. How did you know this? You will answer, of Captain Napier, at *Siena*. The letter announcing the sad event arrived the next day after I got there. They were on the wing—Mrs. W. Light to Leghorn, to meet Colonel Light, and Captain and Mrs. Napier for Naples; so, all things considered, I determined to quit instanter, instead of adding to the trouble.

"Hope that you have been better than usual, and that the pictures go on well. If you should be passing Queen Anne Street, just say I am well, and in Rome, for I fear young Hakewell has written to his father of my being unwell: and may I trouble you to drop a line into the two-penny post to Mr. C. Heath, 6, Seymour Place, New Pancras Church, or send my people to tell him that, if he has anything to send me, to put it up in a letter (it is the most sure way of its reaching me), directed for me, No. 12, Piazza Mignanelli, Rome, and to which place I hope you will send me a line? Excuse my troubling you with my requests of business. Remember me to all friends. So God bless you. Adieu.

"J. M. TURNER."

"TO FRANCIS CHANTREY, R.A.

"No. 12, PIAZZA MIGNANELLI, ROME,
"*Nov. 6, 1828.*

"MY DEAR CHANTREY,

"I intended long before this (but you will say, 'Fudge!') to have written; but even now very little information have I to give you in matters of Art, for I have confined myself to the painting department at Corso; and having finished *one*, am about the second, and getting on with Lord E.'s, which I began the very first touch at Rome; but as the folk here talked that I would show them *not*, I finished a small three feet four to stop their gabbling. So now to business. Sculpture, of course, first; for it carries away all the patronage, so it is said, in Rome; but all seem to share in the good-will of the patrons of the day. Gott's studio is full. Wyatt and Rennie, Ewing, Buxton, all employed. Gibson has two groups in hand, *Venus and Cupid*; and *The Rape of Hylas*, three figures, very forward, though I doubt much if it will be in time (taking the long voyage into the scale) for the Exhibition, though it is for England. Its style is something like *The Psyche*, being two standing figures of nymphs leaning, enamoured, over the youthful Hylas, with his pitcher. The Venus is a sitting figure, with the Cupid in attendance; and if it had wings like a dove, to flee away and be at rest, the rest would not be the worse for the change. Thorwaldsten is closely engaged on the late Pope's (Pius VII.) monument. Portraits of the superior animal, man, is to be found in all. In some, the inferior—viz. greyhounds and poodles, cats and monkeys, &c., &c.

"Pray give my remembrances to Jones and Stokes, and tell *him* I have not seen a bit of coal stratum for months. My love to Mrs. Chantrey, and take the same and good wishes of

"Yours most truly,
"J. M. TURNER."

This method of communicating with "his people" is peculiar, and shows that he was not in the habit of corresponding with them when away on his numerous visits and tours. Perhaps they could not read, perhaps he wished to save postage—whatever hypothesis we may adopt, the fact is singular. The pictures of *The Banks of the Loire*; *The Loretto Necklace*; *Messieurs les Voyageurs on their return from Italy (par la Diligence) in a snowdrift upon Mount Tarra, 22nd of January, 1829*—all exhibited in 1829—were the results of this tour, besides some of the pictures of 1830, one of which, *View of Orvieto*, is, according to Mr. Hamerton, the identical "small three feet four" which he painted to "stop the gabbling" of the folk at Rome.

In this year (1830, he being then fifty-five years old) died Sir Thomas Lawrence, whose loss he probably felt much, and of whose funeral he painted a picture (from memory); but the year had a greater sorrow for him than this—the loss of his "poor old Dad." The removal from Twickenham did not avail to preserve the old man's life for long. We have the testimony of the Trimmers, with whom after the event he stayed for a few days for change of scene, that "he was fearfully out of spirits, and felt his loss, he said, like that of an only child," and that he "never appeared the same man after his father's death." To men like Turner, who are not accustomed to express their feelings much, or even to realize them, such blows come with all their natural violence unchecked, unforeseen, unprovided against. It had probably never occurred to him how much his father was to him, how blank a space his loss would make in his narrow garden of human affection. From this time he was to know many losses of old friends, each of which fell heavily upon him, leaving him more lonely than ever. His friends were few, and they dropped one by one, nor is there any evidence to show that their loss was ever lightened by any hope of meeting them again; the lights of his life went out one by one, and left him alone and in the dark. In 1833 Dr. Monro died, in 1836 Mr. Wells, in 1837 Lord Egremont, in 1841 Chantrey, and he was to feel the loss of Mr. Fawkes and Wilkie, and many more before his own time came.

In February, 1830, he wrote to Jones:—

"DEAR JONES—I delayed answering yours until the chance of this finding you in Rome, to give you some account of the dismal prospect of Academic affairs, and of the last sad ceremonies paid yesterday to departed talent gone to that bourn from whence no traveller returns. Alas! only two short months Sir Thomas followed the coffin of Dawe to the same place. We then were his pall-bearers. Who will do the like for me, or when, God only knows how soon! However, it is something to feel that gifted talent can be acknowledged by the many who yesterday waded up to their knees in snow and muck to see the funeral pomp swelled up by carriages of the great, *without the persons themselves.*"

No doubt these deaths set him thinking of his own, and the disposition of his wealth so useless to him, and he probably brooded long over the will that he signed on the 10th of June in the next year (1831). Many excuses have been made for his niggardly habits on the score of the nobleness of mind shown in this document; he screwed and denied himself (we are told) when living, to make old artists comfortable after his death. We are afraid that there is no ground for this charitable view, nor any evidence that he ever denied himself anything that he preferred to hard cash, or that he ever thought of giving it, or any farthing of it, away to anybody, till he had more than he could spend, and was brought by the deaths of his friends to realize that he could not take it with him when he died. Then indeed he disposed of it; but where was the bulk to go? Not to his nearest of kin, whom he had neglected all his life—fifty pounds was enough for uncles, and twenty-five for their eldest sons; not to his mistress or mistresses, who had been devoted to him all his life, or to his children—annuities of ten and fifty pounds were enough for them; but for the perpetuation of his name and fame, as the founder of "Turner's Gift" and the eclipser of Claude.[44]

We do not know when Turner became acquainted with Samuel Rogers; but probably some years before this, as he is named as one of the executors in the will, and the famous illustrated edition of "Italy" was published in 1830, followed by the Poems in 1834. These contain the most exquisite of all the engravings from Turner's vignettes. Exquisite also are most of the drawings, but some of them are spoilt by the capriciousness of their colour, which seems in many cases to have been employed as an indication to the engraver rather than for the purpose of imitating the hues of nature. The most beautiful perhaps of all, *Tornaro's misty brow*, seems to us far too blue, and the yellow of the sky in others is too strong to be probable or even in harmony with the rest of the drawing. It would, however, be difficult to find in the whole range of his works two really greater (though so small in size) than the *Alps at Daybreak*, and *Datur hora quieti*, of which we give woodcuts, losing of course much of the light refinement of the steel plates, but wonderfully true in general effect. The former is as perfect an illustration as possible of the sentiment of Rogers's pretty verses, but it far transcends them in beauty and imagination; the latter is not in illustration of any of the poet's verses, but is a more beautiful poem than ever Rogers wrote.

The illustration from "Jacqueline" which we give, though not so transcendent in imagination, is a scene of extraordinary beauty of rock and torrent, and castle-crowned steep, such as no hand but Turner's could have drawn, while the *Vision* from "The Voyage of Columbus" is equally characteristic, showing how he could make an impressive picture out of the vaguest notions by his extraordinary mastery of light and shade.

In 1833 Turner exhibited his first pictures of Venice, the last home of his imagination. The date of his first visit to the "floating city" is uncertain. There are two series of Venetian sketches in the National Gallery, which mark two distinct impressions. In the first the colour is comparatively sober; the sky is noted as, before all things, a marvellously blue sky; the interest of the painter is in the watery streets, the picturesqueness of corners here and there, in narrow canals and the different-coloured marbles of the buildings; he takes the city in bits from the inside in broad daylight, and they are studies as realistic as he could make them at the time. In the other series the interest of the painter is COLOUR, not of the buildings, but of the sunsets and sunrises, the clouds of crimson and yellow, the water of green, in which the sapphire and the emerald and the beryl seem to blend their hues. The substantial marble, the solid blue sky, the strong light and sharp shadows have melted into visions of ethereal palaces and gemlike colour, like those in the Apocalypse. As he began painting the sea from Vandevelde and nature, so he began painting Venice from Canaletti and nature; but the transition from the studious beginning to the imaginative end was very swift in the latter case. Venice soon became to him the paradise of colour, and he rose to heights of chromatic daring which exceeded anything which even he had scaled before.

LIGHT-TOWERS OF THE HÈVE.
From "Rivers of France."

The time at which we have now arrived was that of his earlier sketches, and he could turn away from Venice and draw with unabated zest the quieter but still lovely scenery of the Seine and the Loire. To 1833-4 and 1835 belong his beautiful series called *The Rivers of France*. Opinions are divided, as usual, as to the truthfulness of his art to the spirit of French scenery, and a comparison between *The Light-towers of the Hève* in our woodcut, and the drawing which he made on the spot (now in the National Gallery) will show how greatly his imagination altered the literal facts of a scene. One who has patiently followed his footsteps in many parts of England and on the Continent testifies to the puzzling effects of Turner's imaginative records. He seeks in vain on the face of the earth the original of Turner's later drawings, but he can never see these drawings without finding all that he has seen. Indeed, to understand them rightly, they must be considered as poems in colour suggested by pictorial recollections of certain scenes on the rivers of France. Most of them are arrangements of blue, red, and yellow, some of yellow and grey, all exquisitely beautiful in arrangement of line and atmospheric effect. Nor has he in any other drawings introduced figures and animals with more skill and beauty of suggestion. The whole series palpitates with living light, although the pigments employed are opaque, and each view charms the sense of colour-harmony, although the colours are crude and disagreeable. It has always appeared wonderful to us that, with his power over water-colours and delight in clear tones, he should have been content to work with such chalky material and impure tints; it is as though he preferred to combat difficulties; but they were drawn to be engraved, and as long as he got his harmonies and his light and shade true we suppose he was content. The great skill with which he could utilize the grey paper on which these drawings were made, leaving it uncovered in the sky and other places where it would serve his purpose, conduced to swiftness of work, and may have been one of his motives. The drawing of Jumièges, of which we give a woodcut, is one of the loveliest of the series, with its mouldering ruin standing out for a moment like a skeleton against the steely cloud, before the fierce storm covers it with gloom.

In these yearly visits to France, Turner was accompanied by Mr. Leitch Ritchie, who supplied the work with some description of the places. They travelled, however, very little together; their tastes in everything but art being exceedingly dissimilar. "I was curious," says his companion, "in observing what he made of the objects he selected for his sketches, and was frequently surprised to find what a forcible idea he conveyed of a place with scarcely a correct detail. His exaggerations, when it suited his purpose to exaggerate, were wonderful—lifting up, for instance, by two or three stories, the steeple, or rather, stunted cone, of a village church—and when I returned to London I never failed to roast him on this habit. He took my remarks in good part, sometimes, indeed, in great glee, never attempting to defend himself otherwise than by rolling back the war into the enemy's camp. In my account of the famous Gilles de Retz, I had attempted to identify that prototype of 'Blue Beard' with the hero of the nursery story, by absurdly insisting that his beard was so intensely black that it seemed to have a shade of blue. This tickled the great painter hugely, and his only reply to my bantering was—his little sharp eyes glistening the while—'Blue Beard! Blue Beard! Black Beard!'"

JUMIÈGES.
From "Rivers of France."

We do not know when Turner became first acquainted with Mr. Munro of Novar, one of the greatest admirers of the artist and collectors of his later works, but it was in 1836 that we first hear of them as travelling together, when, it is said, "a serious depression of spirits having fallen on Mr. Munro," Turner proposed to divert his mind into fresh channels by travel. They went to Switzerland and Italy, and Mr. Munro found that Turner enjoyed himself in his way—a "sort of honest Diogenes way"—and that it was easy to get on very pleasantly with him "if you bore with his way," a description which, meant to be kind, does not say much for his sociability at this period.

Indeed, he had been all his life, and especially, we expect, since he left Twickenham, developing as an artist and shrivelling as a man, and after this year (1836), though he still developed in power of colour and painted some of his finest and most distinctive works, the signs of change, if not of decline, were also visible. He was also getting out of the favour of the public, who could not see any beauty in such works as the *Burning of the Houses of Lords and Commons*, of 1835, or *Juliet and her Nurse*, of 1836.

FIGHTING TÉMÉRAIRE.
Exhibited in 1839. National Gallery.

His fame began to oscillate, tottering with one picture and set upright by another. As long, however, as he could paint such pictures as *Mercury and Argus*, 1836, and the *Fighting Téméraire*, of 1839, it was in a measure safe. He was still a great genius to whom eccentricities were natural, but the *Fighting Téméraire* was the last picture of his at which no stone was thrown. This is in many ways the finest of all his pictures. Light and brilliant yet solemn in colour; penetrated with a sentiment which finds an echo in every heart; appealing to national feeling and to that larger sympathy with the fate of all created things; symbolic, by its contrast between the old three-decker and the little steam-tug, of the "old order," which "changeth, yielding place to new"—the picture was and always will be as popular as it deserves. It is characteristic of Turner that the idea of the picture did not originate with him, but with Stanfield. Would that Turner had always had some friend at his elbow to hold the torch to his imagination.

CHAPTER VIII.

LIGHT AND DARKNESS.

1840 TO 1851.

THE was now sixty-five years old, and his decline as an artist was to be expected from failing health and stress of years. For little less than half a century he had worked harder and produced more than any other artist of whom we have any record. Nor would he rest now, although his failing powers of body and mind required stimulants to support their energy.

Mr. Wilkie Collins informed Mr. Thornbury that, when a boy—

"He used to attend his father on varnishing days, and remembers seeing Turner (not the more perfect in his balance for the brown sherry at the Academy lunch) seated on the top of a flight of steps, astride a box. There he sat, a shabby Bacchus, nodding like a Mandarin at his picture, which he, with a pendulum motion, now touched with his brush and now receded from. Yet, in spite of sherry, precarious seat, and old age, he went on shaping in some wonderful dream of colour; every touch meaning something, every pin's head of colour being a note in the chromatic scale."

We have spoken of Turner as declining as an artist, but we are not sure that he did so till about 1845, when, Mr. Ruskin says, "his health, and with it in great degree his mind, failed suddenly." Down to this time his decay seems to us to have been more physical than artistic, but with the physical weakness there had been, we think, for some time a deterioration of the non-artistic part of his mind. His decay, though so unlike the decay of others, appears to us to have nothing inexplicable about it if we consider him as a man who had never had any sympathy with the current opinions and culture of his fellows, and who, by some strange defect in his organization, was unable to think without the use of his eyes. That his eyesight failed there is no doubt, but that it did not fail in the one most essential point for a painter, viz., perception of colour, is, we think, proved by his latest sketches in water-colour, which show none of that apparently morbid love of yellow which appears in his later oil pictures, and testify to that perfect perception of the relations and harmonies of different hues which can only belong to a healthy sight. Instead of declining, this faculty of colour seems to have increased in perfection almost to the last. If we compare the sketch in the National Gallery of a scene on the Lake of Zug, done between 1840 and 1845, with one of the 'Rivers of England' *Dartmouth*, two drawings wonderfully alike in composition and in general scheme of colour, no difference in this faculty can be observed; the later drawing is only a few notes higher in the scale. As Mr. Ruskin says, "The work of the first five years of this decade is in many respects supremely and with *reviving* power, beautiful."

But still the decline of his non-artistic mind, never very powerful, had been going on for years, or at least such reasoning power as he possessed had exercised less and less control over the imperious will of his genius, which impelled him to pursue his efforts to paint the unpaintable. He had begun by imitation, he had gone on by rivalry, he had achieved a style of his own by which he had upset all preconceived notions of landscape painting, and had triumphed in establishing the superiority of pictures painted in a light key, but he was not content. His progress had always been towards light even from the earliest days, when he worked in monochrome. Sunlight was his discovery, he had found its presence in shadow, he had studied its complicated reflections, before he commenced to work in colour. From monochrome he had adopted the low scale of the old masters, but into it he carried his light; the brown clouds, and shadows, and mists, had the sun behind them as it were in veiled splendour. Then it came out and flooded his drawings and his canvasses with a glory unseen before in art. But he must go on—refine upon this—having eclipsed all others, he must now eclipse himself. His gold must turn to yellow, and yellow almost into white, before his genius could be satisfied with its efforts to express pure sunlight.

So he went on to his goal, becoming less "understanded of the people" each year, painting pictures more near to the truth of nature in sun and clouds, and less true in everything else. But it was about the everything else that the people most cared. They did not care for sunlight which blinded them, and to which the truth of figure, and sea, and grass, and stone, had to be sacrificed. They liked pictures which could give them calm enjoyment, records of what they had seen or could imagine, not of what Turner only had seen, and what seemed to them extravagant falsity.

Such, roughly put, was the condition of things when a champion arose to scatter Turner's enemies to the four winds. He, Mr. Ruskin (1836), an undergraduate at Oxford, of the age of seventeen, was one not of "the people," but of those comparatively few lovers of art and colour who saw and appreciated the artistic motives of Turner, and who reverenced, as a revelation of hitherto unrecorded, if not undiscovered, beauties of nature, those pictures at which the world scoffed. We cannot here enter further into the discussion involved, but the attitude of the two parties, the one represented by "Blackwood's Magazine," and the other by "Modern Painters," can be judged by the following extracts. The noble enthusiasm aroused by the treatment of *Juliet and her Nurse* by the critics, had suggested a letter in 1836, which gradually increased into a volume, not published till

1843, and in the meantime the undergraduate had gained the Newdegate, and earned the right to call himself "A Graduate of Oxford" on his title-page.

This is what Maga said in August, 1835, of Turner's picture of *Venice, from the porch of Madonna della Salute*, a picture in his earlier Venetian style:—

"Venice, well I have seen Venice. Venice the magnificent, glorious, queenly, even in her decay—with her rich coloured buildings, speaking of days gone by, reflected in the *green* water. What is Venice in this picture? A flimsy, whitewashed meagre assemblage of architecture, starting off ghostlike into unnatural perspective, as if frightened at the affected blaze of some dogger vessels (the only attempt at richness in the picture). Not Venice, but the boat is the attractive object, and what is to make this rich? Nothing but some green and red, and yellow tinsel, which is so flimsy that it is now cracking..... The greater part of the picture is white, disagreeable white, without light or transparency, and the boats, with their red worsted masts, are as gewgaw as a child's toy, which he may have cracked to see what it was made of. As to Venice, nothing can be more unlike its character."

VENICE. THE DOGANA.
In the National Gallery.

This is what the Graduate of Oxford says, after stating his dissatisfaction with the Venices of Canaletti, Prout, and Stanfield:—

"But let us take with Turner, the last and greatest step of all—thank Heaven we are in sunshine again—and what sunshine! Not the lurid, gloomy, plaguelike oppression of Canaletti, but white flushing fulness of dazzling light, which the waves drink and the clouds breathe, bounding and burning in intensity of joy. That sky—it is a very visible infinity—liquid, measureless, unfathomable, panting and melting through the chasms in the long fields of snow-white flaked, slow-moving vapour, that guide the eye along the multitudinous waves down to the islanded rest of the Euganean hills. Do we dream, or does the white forked sail drift nearer, and nearer yet, diminishing the blue sea between us with the fulness of its wings? It pauses now; but the quivering of its bright reflection troubles the shadows of the sea, those azure fathomless depths of crystal mystery, on which the swiftness of the poised gondola floats double, its black beak lifted like the crest of a dark ocean bird, its scarlet draperies flashed back from the kindling surface, and its bent oar breaking the radiant water into a dust of gold. Dreamlike and dim, but glorious, the unnumbered palaces lift their shafts out of the hollow sea—pale ranks of motionless flame—their mighty towers sent up to heaven like tongues of more eager fire—their grey domes looming vast and dark, like eclipsed worlds—their sculptured arabesques and purple marble fading farther and fainter, league beyond league, lost in the light of distance. Detail after detail, thought beyond thought, you find and feel them through the radiant mystery, inexhaustible as indistinct, beautiful, but never all revealed; secret in fulness, confused in symmetry, as nature herself is to the bewildered and foiled glance, giving out of that indistinctness, and through that confusion, the perpetual newness of the infinite and the beautiful.

"Yes, Mr. Turner, we are in Venice now."

Unfortunately the brave young champion was too late, the eloquent voice that could translate into such glowing words the dumb poetry of Turner's pictures had scarcely made the air of England thrill with its musical enthusiasm when black night fell upon the artist. The sudden snapping of some vital chord, of which that same Graduate of Oxford only last year pathetically wrote, took place, and the glorious sun of his genius disappeared without any twilight; he was dead as an artist, and dying as a man. Neither his work nor his life could be defended any more. But the voice that was raised so late in his honour did not die, its vibrations have lasted from that day to this; and if the champion himself seems to be in some need of a defender now, if mouths that once were full of his praise are silent or raised only for the most part to depreciate, it is only what came to Turner and what comes to all who use their imagination too freely to enforce their convictions. A time must come when the spirit of analysis will eat into the most brilliant rhetoric; the false and true, which combine to make the most beautiful fabric of words, cannot wear equally well. To us it is always painful to differ from Mr. Ruskin, to whom we owe the grasp of so many noble truths, the memories of so many delightful hours; and if a time has come when our faith in his dogmas is not absolute, and we feel that he has misled us and others now and again, we cannot close reference to him and his works in this little book without testifying to the great and noble spirit which pervades his work, and recording our admiration of a life devoted to the service of art and man and God with a passionate purity as rare as it is beautiful.

VENICE, FROM THE CANAL OF THE GIUDECEA.
Exhibited in 1840. South Kensington Museum.

But before night fell, in the interval between 1840 and 1845, Turner painted a few pictures of remarkable beauty both in colour and sentiment—pictures which no other artist could have painted, and which we doubt if he could himself have painted before—pictures generally attempting to realize his later ideal of Venice, which even now, in their wrecked beauty, fascinate all who have patience to look at them, and watch the apparent chaos of yellow and white and purple and grey gradually clear into a vision of ghost-like palaces rising like a dream, from the golden sea. Besides these he painted at least three others of unique power: one a record of what few other men could have had the courage to study or the power to paint; one showing the passion of despair at the loss of an old comrade; and another the boldest attempt to represent abstract ideas in landscape that was ever made. We allude to the *Snowstorm*; *Peace, Burial at Sea*; and *Rain, Steam, and Speed*.

Mr. Hamerton says, in connection with the first of these:—

"Let it not be supposed that these works of Turner's decline, however they may have exercised the wit of critics, and excited the amusement of visitors to the Exhibition, were ever anything less than serious performances for him. The *Snowstorm*, for example (1842), afforded the critics a precious opportunity for the exercise of their art. They called it soapsuds and whitewash, the real subject being a steamer in a storm off a harbour's mouth making signals, and going by the lead. In this instance, nothing could be more serious than

Turner's intention, which was to render a storm as he had himself seen it one night when the 'Ariel' left Harwich. Like Joseph Vernet, who, when in a tempest off the island of Sardinia, had himself fastened to the mast to watch the effects, Turner on this occasion, 'got the sailors to lash himself to the mast to observe it,' and remained in that position for four hours. He did not expect to escape, but had a curious sort of conscientious feeling, that it was his duty to record his impression if he survived."[45]

Of the second, which was painted to commemorate Wilkie's funeral, it is related that Stanfield complained of the blackness of the sails, and that Turner answered, "If I could find anything blacker than black I'd use it."[46]

The history of his late Swiss sketches and the drawings he made from them has been recently told by Mr. Ruskin in his valuable and interesting notes to his collection of Turner's drawings exhibited last year (1878), and these notes and the almost equally interesting notes of the Rev. W. Kingsley, contained between the same covers, testify not only to the supreme beauty of his later work, but also to the nobler motive which inspired its production, viz. the desire to "record" as far as he could what he had seen after "fifty years' observation." The days of strife and emulation were over, and a humbler, sweeter spirit made him "put forth his full strength to depict nature as he saw it with all his knowledge and experience." Characteristically, as all through his life, this better spirit showed itself rather in his water-colours made for private persons, than in those oils which he exhibited for the judgment of the public.

We wish we had space here for Mr. Ruskin's splendid description of Turner's picture of *Slavers throwing overboard the Dead and Dying*—a work which seems to us to illustrate what we have said of his manner of decline in a remarkable way. There is no doubt about its splendour of colour, the grandeur of its sea, and the force with which its sentiment of horror and wrong and death is conveyed; but it shows a childishness, a want of mental faculties of the simplest kind, which is all the more extraordinary when brought in contrast with such gigantic pictorial power. The sharks are quite unnecessary, the bodies in the water are too many, the absurdity of the chains appearing above it is too gross; the horror is overdone and melodramatic, or, in a word, one of his finest pictorial conceptions is spoilt for want of a little common sense, of a little power to place himself in relation to his fellows and see how it would appear to them. Again, we cannot help wishing that he had had a friend at his elbow like Stanfield, who would have saved him from the laughter of small critics. He was not fit to manage such a work on such a subject by himself.

In his picture of *War—the Exile and the Rock-limpet*, with its extract from the "Fallacies of Hope"—

"Ah! thy tent-formed shell is like
A soldier's nightly bivouac, alone
Amidst a sea of blood . . . .
. . . But can you join your comrades?"

we see the same mental helplessness. It verges on the sublime, it verges on the ridiculous. We should be sorry to call it either; but it is childish—not with the grand simplicity of Blake, but with the confused complicity of Turner. Mr. Ruskin says that Turner tried in vain to make him understand the full meaning of this work, and we are not surprised.

Such pictures as these had occurred now and then all through his career—pictures in which the means employed were utterly inadequate to express the sentiment duly, such as the *Waterloo*,—pictures in which the accumulation of ideas was confused and excessive, as the *Phryne going to the Bath as Venus, Demosthenes taunted by Æschines*; and he had shown some hazy symbolism in connection with shell-fish in these verses:—

"Roused from his long contented cot he went
Where oft he laboured, and the . . . . bent,
To form the snares for lobsters armed in mail;
But men, more cunning, over this prevail,

THE SLAVE SHIP.
In the possession of Miss Alice Hooper, of Boston, U.S.

Lured by a few sea-snail and whelks, a prey
That they could gather on their watery way,
Caught in a wicker cage not two feet wide,
While the whole ocean's open to their pride."

But now these "failures," for failures they were, however fine the art qualities they possessed, became chronic, and the rule rather than the exception; and this is to us the greatest tragedy in the whole of his career—the spectacle of a great painter, the very slave of his genius, compelled to paint this and paint that at its bidding without being able to distinguish between what was great and what was little, what sublime and what ridiculous, almost as mighty as Milton and Shelley one moment, and as poor as Blackmore or Robert Montgomery the next. He appears to us in these last days like a great ship, rudderless, but still grand and with all sails set, at the mercy of the wind, which played with it a little while and then cast it on the rocks.

Rudderless, masterless, was he also as a man. We are very loth to believe the terrible picture of moral degradation supplied by the "best authority" to Mr. Thornbury, and quoted in the first chapter of this volume; but there is no doubt that he lived by no means a reputable life in his old age. As to how he met with Mrs. Booth, at whose little house by the side of the Thames, near Cremorne, he lived for some time before his death, we have not cared to inquire, nor do we intend to repeat the usual stories about it; nor will we venture an opinion as to how often he took too much to drink or what was his favourite stimulant, or what other excesses he committed. His whole faculties had been absorbed in his art; and when this failed him—when he became broken in health and failing in sight—he had no store of wise reflection to employ his mind, no harmless pursuits to follow, no refined tastes to amuse him, nor, as far as we know, had he any hope of any future rectification of the unevennesses of this world. Some of his friends he had lost by death, many were still living and ready to cheer his last years if he would have had them, but he would not. His secretiveness and love of solitude clung to him to the last.

He did not, however, lose his love of art and his desire of acquiring knowledge relating to it. It was in these last years, 1847-49, that he paid several visits to the studio of Mr. Mayall, the celebrated photographic artist, passing himself off as a Master in Chancery, and taking very great interest in the development of the new process which had not then got beyond the daguerreotype. To the interesting account of these visits printed by Mr. Thornbury,[47] we are enabled by Mr. Mayall's kindness to add that at a time when his finances were at a very low ebb in consequence of litigation about patent rights, Turner unasked, brought him a roll of bank-notes, to the amount of £300, and gave it him on the understanding that he was to repay him if he could. This, Mr. Mayall was able to do very soon, but that does not lessen the generosity of Turner's act.

Notwithstanding, however, such bright glimpses as this, his last years must have been sad and dull, and his greatest source of happiness was probably the knowledge that whatever critics might say of his later works, there were a few men like Mr. Munro, Mr. Griffiths, the Ruskins, father and son, who appreciated them, and that his earlier pictures not only kept up their fame but rose in price. Though in decline, his fame was as great as almost he could have wished. Two offers of £100,000 he is said to have refused for the contents of Queen Anne Street; £5,000 for his two *Carthages*. The greatest of all his triumphs was perhaps when he was waited upon by Mr. Griffiths, with an offer from a distinguished Committee, among whom were Sir Robert Peel, Lord Hardinge, and others, to buy these pictures for the nation. This is the greatest instance of his self-sacrifice, which is well attested; for he refused to part with them because he had willed them to the nation. He might have got the money and his wish also, but he refused. The recollection of this, though it occurred some years before he died, should have afforded him some pleasant reflections.

It had been long known that Turner had another home than that in Queen Anne Street, and he had shown considerable ingenuity in concealing it, for he used to go out of an evening to dinner with his friends when he so willed, and met them at the Academy and other places. Almost to the last he could be merry and sociable at such gatherings, and there is a very pleasant account of a dinner in 1850 at David Roberts' house, given in a note to Ballantyne's life of that artist, at which Turner was. It is a memorandum by an artist from the country, and describes Turner's manner as—

"Very agreeable, his quick bright eye sparkled, and his whole countenance showed a desire to please. He was constantly making or trying to make jokes; his dress, though rather old-fashioned, was far from being shabby." Turner's health was proposed by an Irish gentleman who had attended his lectures on perspective, on which he complimented the artist. "Turner made a short reply in a jocular way, and concluded by saying, rather sarcastically, that he was glad this honourable gentleman had profited so much by his lectures as thoroughly to understand perspective, for it was more than he did." Turner afterwards, in Roberts' absence, took the chair, and, at Stanfield's request, proposed Roberts' health, which he did, speaking hurriedly, "but soon ran short of words and breath, and dropped down on his chair with a hearty laugh, starting up again and finishing with a 'hip, hip, hurrah!'.... Turner was the last who left, and Roberts accompanied him along the street to hail a cab.... At this time Turner was indulging in the singular freak of living, under the name of Mr. Booth, in a small lodging on the banks of the Thames.... This, though now cleared up, was a mystery to his friends then, and Roberts was anxious to unravel it. When the cab drove up he assisted Turner to his seat, shut the door, and asked where he should tell cabby to take him; but Turner was not to be caught, and, with a knowing wink, replied, 'Tell him to drive to Oxford Street, and then I'll direct him where to go.'"

Turner not only kept his secret from his friends, but from Mrs. Danby, who, says Mr. Thornbury—

"One day, as she was brushing an old coat of Turner's, in turning out a pocket, she found and pounced on a letter directed to him, and written by a friend who lived at Chelsea. Mrs. Danby, it appears, came to the conclusion that Turner himself was probably at Chelsea, and went there to seek for him, in company with another infirm old woman. From inquiries in a place by the river-side, where gingerbread was sold, they came to the conclusion that Turner was living in a certain small house close by, and informed a Mr. Harpur,[48] whom she and Turner knew. He went to the place and found the painter sinking. This was on the 18th of December, 1851, and on the following day Turner died."

So died the great solitary genius, Turner, the first of all men to endeavour to paint the full power of the sun, the greatest imagination that ever sought expression in landscape, the greatest pictorial interpreter of the elemental forces of nature, that ever lived. His life, and character, and art, complex as they were in their manifestation, were as simple in motive as those of the most ordinary man. Art, fame, and money were what he strived for from the beginning to the end of his days, and those days were embittered at the end by fallacies of hope with regard to all three. Critics laughed at him, he was given no social honour, (neither knighted nor made President of the Royal Academy), and his money was useless. For the meanness and isolation of his existence he had no one to thank but himself, but this was also, as we hope we have shown in the course of these pages, the natural result of the motives of his life.

THE ROOM IN WHICH TURNER DIED.

The nobleness of his life consisted in his devotion to landscape art, and this should cover many sins. He found it sunk very low: he left it raised to a height which it had never attained before. That he could have done this by painting falsely is absurd. The falsity of his works is just of that kind which comes from almost infinite knowledge of truth. He knew little else but art and nature, and he knew these by heart. He could make nature, and this confidence in his creative power led him sometimes into strange errors, which no one else could have made, such as putting the sun and moon in impossible positions in the same picture, and making boats sail in opposite directions before the wind; but how much more truth of natural phenomena has he not given even in such pictures than can be found in any literal transcript of nature! His colour appears to many to be untrue; but this is greatly due to his clinging from first to last to one central truth—the sun. It was that which gave the pitch to his light, and his colour too, as in nature. To that great light all must be subservient; it is not the local colour of an object in the foreground, or the strength of shade of a particular cave, that controls the chiaroscuro and colouring of nature, but the sun. So all things were sacrificed to this; the green must go from the grass, and the shadows must become scarlet, rather than this truth should be lost. His preference for harmonies of blue, red, and yellow, to the exclusion of green, never giving, as Mr. Leslie pointed out, the "verdure" of England, is remarkable; he is the only artist we know who, instead of the usual "bit of red," to correct the green of a landscape, introduces a bit of "green" (generally harsh crude green), to correct its too great redness. (See, for instance, the apron of the woman in the left-hand corner of his drawing of Rouen Cathedral for the "Rivers of France.") His constant fault, and, as we think, an inexcusable one, is the careless drawing of his figures. It is not an excuse to say that they must not be painted so as to draw attention from the landscape; first, because Turner in his earlier pictures showed that he could introduce well-finished figures without doing this; and secondly, because Turner's figures in his later pictures do this by their badness. This carelessness gradually grew on him, because he would not take pains with them. He could draw very small figures very well, giving more spirit and essence than any other artist, in a touch. He could indicate a shamble, a strut, a march, lassitude, confidence, any physical or mental quality of a figure as easily as he could a bough or a cloud; but when he had to draw a figure to which time must be given, to perfect a definite, complex, organized form, he scamped it. His indication of the spirit of animals is often wonderful, as in the deer in *Arundel Park*, and the dogs in *Troyes*.

Of Turner's mind and character apart from his art not much can be said in praise. The former we have already said so much about that we need only say here that although not of a very high order, except in sensibility and perception, he showed now and then capacities which might have been turned to good account by more generous training. Although his jokes were mainly practical, or of that kind which is understood by the term "waggery;" a few good things which he said have been reported, such for instance as that "indistinctness was his forte;" and though his poetry is generally miserable, it here and there contains a fine expression. It is remarkable, however, how both his wit, and what is good in his poetry, are connected with his art. He never said a thing worth recording about anything else, and the few good bits in his poetry are all reflections of a pictorial image. The utter helplessness of his mind, when he tried to put his reasoning into words, is shown by Mr. Hamerton, in one wonderful extract. (See his "Life of Turner," p. 143.) We do not wonder that his attempts at teaching (though he is said at one time in his youth to have got as much as a guinea a lesson) and his lectures as a professor of perspective were failures.

As to his character, it was mainly negative, on all points except art and money. The best part of it was the tenderness of his heart; but though we have no doubt about this fact, or that he could occasionally in his later years be generous even in money,[49] this does not raise our opinion of him much, for he had more than he wished to spend. If he was remarkable for kind and generous impulses, he was still more remarkable for the success with which he, in general, controlled them. We cannot dispute Mr. Ruskin's assertion that he never "failed in an undertaken trust," but we have yet to learn that he ever undertook one.

If it be really true that, unasked and without any question of repayment, he gave a sum of many thousand pounds on more than one occasion to the son of one of his friends and patrons, such an act deserves more accurate record and complete proof. The money was repaid in both cases, it is said.

He showed his best disposition in his kindness to children and animals, and his fellow-artists. Of the last he always spoke kindly, and to young or old was ever just and kind and patient. Poor Haydon said that he "did him justice;" he assisted many a young man with a useful hint, and once took down one of his pictures at the Academy to find a place for one of an unknown man. He took great interest in the founding of the Artists' Benevolent Fund, and meant his accumulated wealth to be spent in a home for decayed artists.

There is no doubt that long before he died he felt the uselessness of wealth and a desire to dispose of his own in a good way. The only proof we have of his notions of a good way is his will, and that, as we have already said, is not an unselfish document, and the codicils which he added to it from 1831 to 1849 do not show any increase of unselfishness. On the contrary, he revoked his legacies to his uncles and cousins, and left his finished pictures to form a Turner Gallery, and money to found a Turner medal and a monument to himself in St. Paul's Cathedral.

The will and its codicils were so confused that all the legal ability of England was unable to decide what Turner really wanted to be done with his money, and after years of miserable litigation, during which a large portion of it was wasted in legal expenses, a compromise was effected, in which the wishes of the parties to the suits and others concerned, including the nation and the Royal Academy, were consulted rather than the wishes of the testator: his desire to found a charity for decayed artists, the only thing upon which his mind seems to have been fixed from first to last in these puzzled documents, was over—thrown, and his next of kin, the only persons mentioned in his will whom he certainly did not mean to get a farthing, got the bulk of the property (excepting the pictures). We have no doubt it was quite right; we are very glad the nation got all the pictures and drawings, finished and unfinished, and the Royal Academy £20,000; that there are a Turner medal and a Turner Gallery, and we think that the next of kin should have had a great deal of his money: but surely the greatest fallacy of all Turner's hope was that his will would be construed according to his intentions.

Two of his wishes with regard to himself were, however, fully carried out—his desire to be buried in St. Paul's and the expenditure of £1,000 on his monument. His funeral was conducted with considerable pomp and ceremony, his "gifted talents," to use his own words, "acknowledged by the many," and many of his fellow-artists and admirers followed him to the grave; nor amongst the crowd were wanting a few old friends who in their hearts still cherished him as "dear old Turner."

"DATUR BORA QUIETI."

FOOTNOTES:

[1] "Absalom and Achitophel."

[2] Mr. Cyrus Redding met him there in 1812, and Sir Charles Eastlake then or after then. There is no engraved drawing by him from Devonshire till the *Southern Coast*, which began in 1814, or picture, till the *Crossing of the Brook*, exhibited in 1815.

[3] Mr. Thornbury treats this as an absurd tradition, but it is supported by an account given by Dr. Shaw of an interview between him and the artist, and printed by Mr. T. pp. 318, 319. "May I ask you if you are the Mr. Turner who visited at Shelford Manor, in the county of Nottingham, in your youth?" "I am," he answered. On being further questioned as to whether his mother's name was Marshall, he grew very angry, and accused his visitor of taking "an unwarrantable liberty," but was pacified by an apology, and invited Dr. Shaw to give him "the favour of a visit" whenever he came to town.

[4] He was called "William" at home.

[5] See "Notes and Queries," 2nd series, v. 475, for the true version of this story.

[6] Wornum.

[7] Dr. Thomas Monro, of Bushey and Adelphi Terrace, physician of Bridewell and Bethlehem Hospitals, a well-known lover of art and patron of Edridge, Girtin, Turner, W. Hunt, and other young artists. He erected monuments at Bushey Church to Edridge and Hearne.

[8] This gentleman is described by Mr. Thornbury as Mr. *Harraway*, a *fish*monger in Broad*way*.

[9] This took place in 1836.

[10] Mr. John Britton, publisher, and author of "Beauties of Wiltshire," &c., &c.

[11] Perhaps the Earl of Essex.

[12] See Memoir prefixed to "Liber Fluviorum."

[13] "Turner and Girtin's Picturesque Views," London, 1854.

[14] See also Mr. Wedmore's interesting essay on Girtin for a story about Turner and Girtin's drawing of the *White House at Chelsea*.

[15] Whether father or son does not appear.

[16] Down to 1851 the Exhibition, in common parlance, always meant the Exhibition of the Royal Academy.

[17] His first exhibited oil picture, according to Mr. S. Redgrave. See "Dictionary of Artists of the English School."

[18] According to most accounts his first exhibited oil picture.

[19] See Whitaker's "Parish of Whalley," vol. ii. p. 183.

[20] See also Willis's "Current Notes" for Jan. 1852.

[21] In a letter from Andrew Caldwell to Bishop Percy, dated 14th June, 1802, printed by Nicholls in his "Illustrations of the Literary History of the Eighteenth Century," vol. viii. p. 43, Turner is spoken of as beating "Loutherbourg and every other artist all to nothing." "A painter of my acquaintance, and a good judge, declares his pencil is magic; that it is worth every landscape-painter's while to make a pilgrimage to see and study his works. Loutherbourg, he used to think of so highly, appears now mediocre."

[22] The names of these pictures are given as printed in the Catalogue.

[23] Rawlinson.

[24] See saying of Turner's reported by Mr. Halstead, and printed in note in Mr. Rawlinson's "Turner's Liber Studiorum, Macmillan and Co., 1878," from which excellent work most of the above information is derived.

[25] Not issued till the 10th part, or over five years from the publication of the first.

[26] Only a portion of it, the picture.

[27] The only picture exhibited at the Academy by this artist. It was called *A Landscape, with Hannibal in his March over the Alps, showing to his Army the Fertile Plains of Italy*. As its year of exhibition was 1776, it would be interesting to learn where Turner saw this picture. Where is it now? Our information on the subject is derived from Redgrave's "Century of Painters."

[28] Thornbury, p. 236.

[29] He became Professor of Perspective to the Royal Academy in this year.

[30] Turner seems to have paid a visit to the Continent in 1804, as Mr. Thornbury refers to some powerful water-colour Swiss scenes of 1804 at Farnley, p. 240.

[31] There is no record of a visit by Turner to the Isle of Man.

[32] Wordsworth's "Elegiac Stanzas," suggested by a picture of 'Peele Castle in a storm,' painted by Sir George Beaumont.

[33] "Past Celebrities," by Cyrus Redding, vol. i.

[34] Thornbury, p. 152.

[35] See Wornum, "Turner Gallery," p. xv., for a Catalogue of Turner's Gallery in 1809.

[36] He is said to have been his own architect for both houses.

[37] See Thornbury, p. 224.

[38] See Thornbury, p. 223.

[39] Called in the Catalogue *Whitehall Stairs, June 18th, 1817.*

[40] *Helvoetsluys: the City of Utrecht, 64, going to sea.*

[41] Turner had a picture of the same subject in another room. The two artists had agreed together that each should paint it.

[42] Leslie's "Autobiographical Recollections," vol. i. pp. 202, 203.

[43] They are printed as given by Thornbury.

[44] In his first will he only leaves two pictures to the Nation, the *Sun Rising through Mist* and the *Carthage*, and on condition that they were to be hung side by side with the great Claudes.

[45] Hamerton, pp. 286-87.

[46] Ibid., p. 292.

[47] Thornbury, pp. 349-51.

[48] Mr. Harpur, the grandson of the sister of his mother, one of his executors.

[49] We are informed by Mr. J. Beavington Atkinson, to whom we are indebted for other interesting facts in connection with Turner, that he was not ungrateful to his early friends, the Narraways of Bristol, but supplied them from time to time with sums of money, and that at his death there was a sum owing by one of the family who wished to repay it, but was informed by the executors that Turner had left no record of any such debt.

Milton Keynes UK
Ingram Content Group UK Ltd.
UKHW031300251024
450245UK00004B/413